JUSTICE
AND WAR
IN THE
NUCLEAR AGE

Robert R. Reilly
Rev. James V. Schall, S.J.
Thomas F. Payne
Angelo Codevilla
Most Rev. John J. O'Connor
Philip F. Lawler, Editor

American Catholic Committee

UNIVERSITY
PRESS OF
AMERICA

JUSTICE AND WAR IN THE NUCLEAR AGE

Robert R. Reilly
Rev. James V. Schall, S.J.
Thomas F. Payne
Angelo Codevilla
Most Rev. John J. O'Connor
Philip F. Lawler, Editor

American Catholic Committee

UNIVERSITY
PRESS OF
AMERICA

LANHAM • NEW YORK • LONDON

University Press of America,™ Inc.

4720 Boston Way
Lanham, MD 20706

3 Henrietta Street
London WC2E 8LU England

Library of Congress Catalog Card Number: 83-45031

Table of Contents

Preface

The papers contained in this volume were presented (some in abbreviated form) at a conference in Washington, D.C., sponsored by the American Catholic Committee, on October 16, 1982. For help in making that conference possible, the American Catholic Committee is grateful to the National Strategy Information Center, and to The Heritage Foundation. The production and distribution of this book were made possible by the Catholic Center for Renewal.

The American Catholic Committee was founded early in 1982 by a group of Catholic laymen concerned about the misinterpretation of Catholic teachings, especially on social and political issues. All of the organization's functions are performed by volunteers, with the support provided by membership dues and private contributions. For further information, contact the editor at 226 Massachusetts Avenue, N.E., Suite 22, Washington, D.C. 20002.

This conference on Justice and War in the Nuclear Age, and this publication, would not have been possible without the dedication of many members of the A.C.C.. In particular, Robert Reilly was responsible for the overall coordination of the conference. Catherine Barr handled publicity and invitations. And in New York, James McFadden ploughed through the mounds of mail generated by the conference.

Although they do not appear in this volume, two other conference speakers deserve mention. Former National Security Adviser Richard Allen delivered the luncheon address, and Hon. Frank Shakespeare contributed a moving speech for the dinner audience. Unfortunately, both of those addresses were delivered *ex tempore*, and no record of their remarks remains.

About the Authors

Philip F. Lawler, the editor of this volume, is the President of the Catholic Center for Renewal, and director of studies at The Heritage Foundation. He is the author of, among other works, *The Bishops and the Bomb.*

Robert R. Reilly, the organizer of this conference, is Director of Private Sector Programs for the U.S. Information Agency. He has in the past been an Army lieutenant, a national director of the Intercollegiate Studies Institute, and a director of government information for The Heritage Foundation.

Rev. James V. Schall, S.J. is a professor of government at Georgetown University, and has served as a consultor to the Pontifical Commission on Justice and Peace. He is the author of several books, including *Liberation Theology and Politics* and *Church, State, and Society in the Thought of John Paul II.*

Thomas Payne, educated at Notre Dame and Claremont, is a professor of political science at Hillsdale College in Michigan. In addition to his scholarly publications, he has written editorial columns syndicated through Public Research Syndicate.

Angelo Codevilla is a staff member of the Senate Select Committee on Intelligence, a lecturer at Georgetown University, and a lieutenant commander in the naval reserve. A former Hoover Institution scholar, he is the author of several books and numerous articles on international politics and intelligence.

Most Rev. John J. O'Connor is auxiliary bishop of New York and Vicar General for the U.S. Military Vicariate. Ordained in Philadelphia in 1945, he entered the Navy as a chaplain in 1952 and remained in the service until 1979, reaching the rank of Rear Admiral and chief of chaplains. Pope John Paul II consecrated him a bishop in 1979. He is the author of *A Chaplain Looks at Vietnam* and *In Defense of Life.*

Introduction

Philip F. Lawler

Late in 1982, as the American Catholic bishops prepared to debate the question of nuclear armament, the heated political debates deflected attention from a long, solid tradition of Catholic thought on such issues. The essays contained in this volume, commissioned by the American Catholic Committee in October 1982, are intended to restore attention to that tradition. Although these essays will certainly prove informative to anyone studying the current controversy, they should be equally valuable after the debate dies down. The political issues of the moment come and go, but the Just War tradition has remained powerful for almost 1500 years.

The crucial ingredients of any distinctively Catholic debate on armaments—nuclear or otherwise—remain constant: a dispassionate use of reason to assess practical options, a reliance on the traditional teachings of the Church and its scholarly representatives, a faith in the power of prayerful reflection, and above all an insistence that the life of the soul is the most important of all human values. The essays contained in this book emphasize the tradition of reason, but they are all founded on a prior commitment to the place of prayer in resolving international problems. Our Lord Jesus is the Prince of Peace, but that peace is not of this world—not a matter simply of stopping the armed conflicts among nations. Conflicts will continue, and armaments will threaten, until all nations are reconciled in Christ. And since the causes of war are always found in the hearts of men, the Catholic's final resource for peace lies in the power of prayer, not politics.

Still, political answers can contribute to the struggle for peace, and the struggle to make war less likely and less horrible. In that context, the controversy surrounding the bishops' Pastoral Letter on War and Peace takes on special significance. Have the "peace bishops" politicized the Gospel? Have they drifted away from the healthy traditions of Catholic teachings on war and justice? A few of these bishops explicitly deny the relevance of the Just War tradition in a nuclear age; it is not clear whether they understand the tradition that they are condemning. Nor is it clear that the bishops and their many supporters, in their quest for a new initiative toward peace, have dissected all the consequences of their proposed stance. The drive toward peacemaking is powered by the most admirable of motives, but it can be derailed quickly if it is not also guided by the cold reason that questions every suggestion for its practical implications.

Moreover, the initiatives of the "peace bishops" are often misinterpreted by the secular media, so that the American public receives a grossly distorted view of the Catholic teachings. Bishops, like all other specialists, speak a language that outsiders often do not understand. And political ideologues, both within the Church and within the media, seize upon a few Church pronouncements to use them for their own political purposes. News reports, written under the press of time and space, rarely provide enough background to help people understand the intellectual origins of the Church teachings; nor do they explain the subtleties of a tradition which is, after all, grounded in transcendental truths. So press reports distort the Church position. And if one set of ideological crusaders monopolize the public discussion, the distortion quickly grows.

Thus the American Catholic Committee saw in the nuclear-arms debate a prime example of the misinterpretation of Catholic teachings, and a prime topic for a more balanced presentation. The activism of a few bishops and clerics, combined with the distortions engendered by the media, have caused a widening split within the Church: a split between the perceptions of the ordinary laymen and the statements of some visible Church spokesmen. These essays constitute an effort to repair that split, by articulating the thoughts and fears of thousands of faithful Catholics. On questions of doctrine, Catholics owe their allegiance to their bishops. But on questions of political analysis, the bishops should hear out the views of laymen who have a special expertise in that field. As history amply demonstrates, bishops have no special ability to analyze political problems.

The political problems involved in nuclear weaponry are both important and complex. Everyone agrees on the basic question: the cause of peace is unopposed. But how can one best pursue peace? Modern weaponry comes in a wide variety of forms, and strategies vary accordingly. Are all modern weapons equally subject to the same moral guidelines? It would seem quite implausible that there are no relevant distinctions to be made. And since men, not weapons, cause war, is it not our primary responsibility to speak about strategies and intentions rather than about missiles and bombs?

On many other questions, the teachings of the Church must be conjoined with some hard strategic analysis before any moral judgments are possible. For instance:

1. If we reject the doctrine of Mutually Assured Destruction (as all the authors in this volume do), are we left with any other plausible basis for a strategy of nuclear deterrence? Would such a new strategy incur the same moral objections?

2. What are the practical consequences of various arms-control suggestions? Would a decrease in nuclear weapons lead to an increase in conventional armament? If we make nuclear war less likely, do we simultaneously make conventional war more likely, and even more deadly?

3. How can we gauge the comparative risks of different defense postures? Since World War II, we have seen no nuclear exchanges, but hundreds of conventional wars. Does it make sense to concentrate our energies on eliminating the danger that has—to this date—proved more remote?

4. Scientific breakthroughs at any moment could render nuclear weapons obsolete. Will technology provide answers to our moral questions, or will warfare become even more terrifying? Can we promote the development of more acceptable weaponry and strategy?

5. In condemning modern warfare, the Vatican Council referred not to nuclear devices, but to "weapons of mass destruction." Do all nuclear weapons fall under that ban? Are some nuclear devices less destructive than their conventional counterparts?

The list of such questions could be extended indefinitely, and indeed many other equally vexing questions are raised in the essays that follow. The authors present a variety of differing views; they do not always agree with each other. But they do attempt to grapple with the most difficult themes, and introduce readers to the most prominent lines of analysis. As a guide to further study and reflection, this volume contains an annotated listing of other sources that might help the serious reader to complete his education on this question.

These essays are not light reading, nor are they intended to be. The Catholic tradition of analysis on this vital question has been developed for hundreds of years, and the intellectual content of the discussion has become progressively higher with each generation of scholars. Anyone who seeks an accurate understanding of the Church teaching—as opposed to the simplistic formulae that make headlines today—cannot avoid some very serious study.

The challenge confronting the Catholic Church today is to apply this tradition productively to the contemporary American political scene. The bishops, in their Pastoral Letter, can indulge themselves in utopian thinking, or they can apply themselves to a more selective critique of our national defense posture. If they choose the former path, they will isolate themselves not only from their followers but also from their potential audience in Washington; they will become irrelevant. But if they choose the latter path, they can make an enormous contribution to our national debate—a contribution that could not come from any other source. No one is totally satisfied with our strategic posture today. The question, however, is how it can be changed without damaging our security. The situation calls for careful, subtle analysis—not for blanket condemnations and moral posturing.

Our nation needs a new strategic doctrine: a doctrine that would retain the security of nuclear deterrence without relying on the horrible threat of massive destruction. We need a defense force that will discourage aggressors at all levels—not merely on the strategic nuclear level—without increasing the dangers of war. We need a deterrent in which our preparations match our risks, and our potential for destruction is proportionate to the evils we seek to avoid. In short, we need to construct a defensive posture based on the predicates of the Just War tradition. If the bishops advance the argument in that direction, they will have done an enormous service for the cause of peace.

At the same time, the bishops cannot represent the Church adequately without emphasizing the prior importance of spiritual help in our quest for peace. A nation's defensive capacities can make war less likely, or less horrible. But no earthly defense can make war impossible, because no earthly defense can resolve the conflicts among men. There is no political formula that can ensure peace.

There is, however, a spiritual formula, amply explained in Scripture and in the teachings of the Church. Conversion and reconciliation are processes of grace, not of practical politics. So in the battle for peace, we as Christians should rely most heavily on our one unanswerable weapon: prayer.

Philip F. Lawler
Washington, D.C.
October, 1982

The Nature of Today's Conflict

Robert R. Reilly

We can begin with the question as it was put by Father John Courtney Murray, S.J.:

"What precisely are the values, in what hierarchical scale, that today are at stake in the international conflict? What is the degree of danger in which they stand? What is the mode of the menace itself—in particular, to what extent is it military and to what extent is it posed by forms of force that are more subtle? If these questions are not carefully answered, one will have no standard against which to match the evils of war. And terror, rather than reason, will command one's judgments. . ."[1]

When a mind is terrorized, it is incapable of moral reasoning. This is the great danger of the hysteria created by the apocalyptic pronouncements of the peace movement. We are told that the mass destruction of humanity is the only alternative to disarmament, and that nuclear exchange of any kind must be avoided at any price. In other words, nothing worth defending could require a nuclear defense. However, this is the abdication of moral reasoning, for it makes it impossible to answer Fr. Murray's question: What *values* are at stake in the conflict? To say that this question and the answers to it are irrelevant in the face of nuclear weapons is to deprive ourselves of the concepts of good and evil. It is unilateral moral disarmament, far worse than the loss of any weapon. As Patrick Glynn said in his review of Jonathan's Schell's *The Fate of the Earth*, "It is not the threat of nuclear war that has trivialized our moral values; rather, it is the gradual loss of faith in any and all values that has rendered the naked possibility of violent death by nuclear war so stark, so threatening, so irreducibly horrifying. . ."[2]

"But," as Solzhenitsyn warns us, "if we are to be deprived of the concepts of good and evil, what will be left? Nothing but the manipulation of one another. We will decline to the status of animals."[3] This, then, is the ultimate price for dismissing the moral character

5

of the conflict—what is morally at stake in it—as superfluous in the face of nuclear terror: it makes the moral character of peace superfluous as well. For in saying that it is worth *any* price to prevent nuclear conflicts, the premise is that "morally and politically, nothing matters—nothing, that is, except survival."[4] As Joseph Cropsey has pointed out, "The proper name for this position is not philanthropic morality, but nihilism without intestines."[5] Since this movement against war does not speak to the moral character of the "peace" following defeat in a war without a nuclear defense or following the consequences of unilateral disarmament, the peace called for seems to be nothing more than the absence of war. But true peace is the result of justice. It is not the absence of something, but a fullness of right order. Justice is the source of peace; injustice the origin of conflict. (And as Pope John Paul II reminded us, "There can be no love without justice.") "Peace" without justice is the continuation of moral violence by other means. This is why Solzhenitsyn said, "the movement 'against war' falls far short of filling the demands of a movement 'for peace,'"[6] because of its acquiescence in the continuation of moral violence. Worse, such movements corrupt the word peace by applying it to this capitulation.

In his first speech before the AFL-CIO on June 30, 1975, Solzhenitsyn gave as an example of moral myopia the headline run in a major newspaper after the US defeat in Southeast Asia. It read: "The Blessed Silence." This is celebrating the silence of the grave. Do the screams of butchered Cambodians make a sound if they are not heard in the West? Apparently not; all is quiet, all is blessed peace. More people have been killed in Southeast Asia since the withdrawal of the United States than during the entire war. Peace be with you? This is the peace brought to Southeast Asia in part by the anti-war movement, a peace worse than war. There were no boat people fleeing Vietnam during the worst of the war; they only fled the peace. Peace be unto you? The incense celebrating this blessed peace is the multi-colored cloud of yellow rain that descends upon Hmong villagers who die from vomiting their own blood. This benediction is now being bestowed upon Afghanistan. This kiss of peace is poisoned. *Pax Sovietica.*

The terrorized mind, then, rejects "peace" as a morally specific form of order for mere survival on any terms.

We can say, then, that Father Murray's questions are legitimate and require answers. They require answers according to the principle of proportion in just war teaching. We must have an accurate idea of what is at stake in a war, otherwise we cannot judge what exertions are justified for defense. The worth of the things to be defended, then, is of critical importance. If greater harm will be caused by their defense than good achieved, then war would not be justified. But, as Father Murray reminds us,

> Pius XII laid some stress on the fact the comparison here must be between realities of the moral order, and not sheerly between two sets of material damage and loss. The standard is not 'eudaemonism and utilitarianism of materialist origin,' which would avoid war merely because it is uncomfortable, or connive at injustice simply because its repression would be costly. The question of proportion must be evaluated in a more tough-minded fashion, from the viewpoint of the hierarchy of strictly moral values. It is not enough simply to consider 'the sorrows and evils that flow from war.' There are greater evils than the physical death and destruction wrought in wars."[7]

What are these evils? Father Murray continues:

> "The tradition of reason has always maintained that the highest value in society is the inviolability of the order of rights and justice. If this order disintegrates or is successfully defied, society is injured in its most vital structure and end. Peace itself is the work of justice, and therefore peace is not compatible with impunity for the evil of injustice."[8]

Pope Pius XII even spoke of the "absolute necessity of self-defense against a very grave injustice that touches the community, that cannot be impeded by other means, that nevertheless must be impeded on pain of giving free field in international relations to brutal violence and lack of conscience."[9] War, he believed, is a moral obligation if employed in a defense against evil, if that evil cannot be stopped by other means. Coming so soon after World War II, there can be little doubt that Pius XII's remarks arose from the experience of Nazi Germany.

Antipathy Between Regimes

The predominant feature of world politics today is the struggle between the United States and the Soviet Union. The question of proportion that we must put to ourselves has been succinctly stated by Joseph Cropsey: "Do we have any reason for believing that the sovietization of the world is an evil commensurate with the peril created by opposing it?"[10] To answer, we must see if this indeed is the objective of our enemy; and we can only judge whether or not it is an evil by examining the moral character of the Soviet Union. Since the question presumes our own extinction as a nation we must also judge our own moral worth and see to what degree our loss would be an evil.

To understand the nature of the Soviet regime requires us to understand the nature of modern ideology of which it is currently the most powerful expression. In his Harvard commencement address, "A World Split Apart," Solzhenitysyn traced the roots of modern ideology to the Renaissance and the Age of Enlightenment, and articulated its two strongest tenets: the "automony of man from any higher force above him" and the refusal to admit to "the existence of intrinsic evil in man."[11] But to understand the background against which modern ideology arose, we have to go back even further to the dawn of philosophy in the Greek world.

Before philosophy, a tribal mentality prevailed. A member of one tribe or city had no conception of a member of another tribe as a fellow human being. This was because he had no idea of what a human being is; he had no conception of human nature. He had a notion of himself only as a tribal member, with duties to his tribal gods and nothing else. To enslave or slaughter a member of another tribe fit perfectly in the order of the tribal view and gods.

Greek philosophy, at the foundation of Western civilization, made a number of momentous discoveries: that the mind can know things, as distinct from having opinions about them; that objective reality exists; that there seems some purpose implied in its construction; and that this purpose has to do with what man called 'the good.' These were all preparations for a greater discovery: Nature, the recognition of which enables man to acknowledge his fellow human beings as members of the same species. This act of the intellect is at the basis of our civilization. We have forever since called barbarian those who are incapable of it.

The very idea of human nature as it came to be articulated in Greek philosophy was that all men are subject to a single standard of justice which transcends tribal differences and time itself. There is not one justice for an Athenian and another for a Spartan, but the same justice for both. This single standard of justice means nothing less than the existence of human nature as universal, immutable, and normative.

The differences between tribes were found by philosophers to be matters of convention, not of nature. In nature men are constituted in the same essential way, their souls directed to the same good grounded in the transcendent order of the divine. Expressed in the religious realm, this meant that there are no tribal gods, but the one true God of all men and of all times.

These revelations of Greek philosophy can be expressed in another way that will show their ultimate relevance to our topic: that the order of the soul and the order of the city (the political order) are not the same; that the one, in fact, transcends the other; that man owes his final allegiance to higher things. In *The Republic*, Plato showed the limits of the political by transposing the order of the soul into the political order and letting us see, in the form of an imaginary state, what such a transposition would mean. He asked, in effect: If we tried to realize politically a perfect state according to the order of the soul, what would we get? The answer was: the garrison state, the destruction of the family, regimentation, the abolition of the private, eugenics, state education, etc. In other words, the political order cannot satisfy the highest needs of man; if it is made the vehicle for doing so, it will end in an horrendous tyrrany. The two orders are not and cannot be coterminous.

The distinction between the two is fundamental to what we have come to call human rights, by which we mean the inviolate order of the soul upon which the state may not trespass. (This creates a certain tension between the two orders; Socrates was its first victim.) The idea of human nature as a metaphysical reality—something giver rather than made by man—and monotheism formed Western civilization, out of which alone came the concern for the sacredness and inviolability of the individual human being. The proper role of politics, according to its vision, is to be limited to the protection of that inviolability by maintaining an order sufficient for the pursuit of man's higher ends.

But what are man's higher ends? If there is a pursuit, what is sought, and why? If the political order cannot meet these needs of the soul, what can? And why does man seek a transformation of himself in the first place?

These questions arise from common experience. In Western civilization, they have received their most comprehensive answer in the Judeo-Christian revelation.

The common experience of man is that he desires happiness, but is unhappy. He feels a keen sense of loss and desolation. He seeks, but finds nothing in this world adequate to his deepest longings. He suffers, and dies. Why is this so? And in what or in whom is man to find the object of his deepest desire; or can it be found? Thus, man has always been confronted with the fact of evil. Even if it is not seen as "evil" per se, everyone admits that there is something radically wrong with the world. The Judeo-Christian tradition shaped the West by assigning the source of that evil to original sin— to a cataclysmic dislocation in the relationship between God and man which resulted in "fallen nature." The essence of that original sin is a disorder within man himself, the preference of oneself to God: pride. (This disorder within man is also the origin of war. As Saint James explains, "What causes war and what causes fightings among you? Is it not your passions that are at war in your members? You desire and do not have; so you kill. And you covet and cannot obtain; so you fight and wage war." James 4:1-2). Salvation—the restoration of the proper God-man relationship—can only be achieved in the sacrifice of Christ by man renouncing evil with good works in cooperation with God's mercy and grace. Salvation is then gained when the good man is united with God in the afterlife.

The purpose of man then was firmly imbedded in the natural and divine order of things. This outlook drew upon the classical belief in a comprehensible, rational world ordered to certain ends, among which was understood to be an end for man in "the good," which the Christian took to be God Himself, in whom man would find his total fulfillment. The Christian view was thus comprehensive: it explained man's origins in God's creation, the existence of evil from original sin, and the final triumph of salvation in Christ over evil and death. Life was understandable in these terms: it had a meaning and purpose with which man could transform his sufferings into something endurable and ultimately salvific. If man could not feel at home here, he had the reassurance that he was meant for elsewhere. "Thou hast made us for Thyself, O Lord, and our hearts are restless until they rest in Thee," said Saint Augustine in his *Confessions*. Man's end, then, was outside of history in personal union with a transcendent and loving God.

Ideology Confronts Religion

Every historical substitution for Christianity, including Soviet ideology, replaces its basic elements: mimics it with an ersatz Paradise from which man fell, an ersatz origin of the fall as the source of evil, and an ersatz plan for salvation. This is, in effect, why modern ideology can only be accurately understood as a pseudo-religion, an ersatz plan for salvation, for the transformation of the world without grace. By removing the locus of man's salvation from the spiritual and transcendent, and placing it within history and the material, it transforms politics into religion and the state into the engine of salvation. This is why the true ideologue exhibits the fervor of a religious zealot; he is busy making the "new" man.

This typology of modern ideology is manifest in its earliest practitioners. We need only look at the thought of Jean Jacques Rousseau to discern its general contours.

By the 18th century, the religious view of the world had seriously eroded. The thought that "sin" was responsible for unhappiness and pain met with skepticism. It was Rousseau who, in his *Discourse on the Origin and Foundation of Inequality Among Men*, made the case, startling even for that time, that society itself was the cause of the evils afflicting man: that before society man lived in an isolated state of nature in which he was perfectly content and happy because the pure "sentiment of his own existence" was so pleasant that "one suffices to oneself, like God."[12] (There could hardly be a more radical assertion of man's independence.) It was only when through some unexplainable "accident" one man was forced into association with another that this godlike automony ended. Due to his increasing contact with other men, man began not to live in his own self-sufficient esteem, but was drawn out of himself to live only in the esteem of others. In this way man was "alienated" from himself and enslaved to others. Here we see in Rousseau the origin of Marx's idea of exploitation, carried through, in our own time, to Sartre's existential assertion that: "Hell is other people."

Nonetheless, Rousseau saw that the blissful isolation and independence of the pre-social state of nature is lost forever, much as was the Garden of Eden. The closest man can come to secular salvation is to abolish those dependent forms of association which have enslaved him to other men and kept him always outside of himself. He must sever, as much as possible, his relations with his fellow members of society so he can return the sentiment of his own existence to himself. How can this be done? Rousseau describes the accomplishment of this condition: "Each person would then be completely independent of all his fellowmen, and absolutely dependent upon the state." Rousseau's program is to politicize society totally and his first target is society's foundation—the primary means by which men are cured of that total self-absorption to which Rousseau wishes them to return—the family.

Rousseau's attack upon the family and his exclusive reliance upon the state as the vehicle of man's redemption is the prototype for all future revolutionaries. The program is always the same: society, responsible for all evils, must be destroyed. To promote universal "brotherhood," the family must be eliminated. Once society is atomized, once the family ceases to interpose between the individual and the state, the state is free to transform the isolated individual by force into whatever version of "new man" the revolutionary visionaries espouse.

Who this new man is to be was made explicit in the 19th century by Nietzsche and Marx. They both spoke in the terms of classical philosophy and metaphysics. They both posed the problem of the human condition in the familiar metaphysical terms of existence and essence. Marx described communism as "the true resolution of the conflict between existence and essence. . . It is the riddle of history solved and knows itself as this solution."[13] Nietzsche saw his task "to impress the character of being [essence] upon becoming [existence]."[14] The problem they referred to is the contingent nature of man: the fact that it is not necessary for man to exist. Man is born, lives and dies. He is transient. Nothing could be clearer to him than that he is dependent upon others for his being. He is not his own cause, and whatever brought him into the world will soon take him out again. In metaphysical terms, he realizes that he does not have existence necessarily because of his essence; rather that his existence is accidental, that he is a contingent, or caused, being. He observes that this, in fact, is true of all things within his experience. Nothing exists necessarily. All things have existence as a result of causes outside themselves. But how can a succession of things that do not exist necessarily *be*? This is Heideger's famous question: Why is there something rather than nothing?[15] It seems more reasonable in a way for there to be nothing.

Quite clearly, the world is not self-explanatory. It is upon this realization, as Father Martin D'Arcy said, "that we must turn to religion,"[16] or at least open ourselves to the possibility of its truth. Arriving at the contingent nature of all that surrounds him, man reasons to the existence of a being that exists necessarily because of its essence, whose essence *is* existence, that is, a being that is its own cause. These are the very terms in which Jahweh introduces Himself in the *Old Testament:* "I Am Who Am." This being, God, provides the ground for all existence, and is the first cause and end of all things. All things are contingent in relation to Him, creations of His will. But this does not explain why He chooses to create anything. The reason God chooses to will things into existence is a mystery, comprehended only through His infinite charity. Or as C.S. Lewis once speculated, it is "to increase the joy."

The modern enterprise tries to solve the problem of human existence, of evil, here in this world, without God. Not having God provides the hope for certain advantages. The great hope of nihilism, as Nietzsche expressed it, is that "man will rise higher when he ceases to flow into God,"[17] that man will become truly himself unfettered by the limits of God and His nature. Ideologues believe in the reverse of the Promethean myth. It is not man who stole fire from the gods, but the gods who stole fire from man. Ideologues aim to get it back by destroying the myth of religion and ending man's alienation by returning to him what is truly his. As Marx said, "The religion of the workers has no God, because it seeks to restore the divinity of man."[18]

But on the basis of what criteria, one may ask, has modern ideology judged the inadequacy of Christianity, of God and His nature? Nietzsche's answer is decisive: "Now, it is our preference that decides against Christianity—not arguments."[21] God's death is willed, not discovered. It is a matter of choice, and it is based upon a deep-seated resentment of what is, of what prevents man himself from being god. "If there were gods in existence," asks Zarathustra, "how could I endure not to be a god?"[19] "We must hate," Lenin counseled, "hatred is the basis of communism."[20] The willful, antirational nature of the enterprise is also apparent in Marx, who forbade his followers from even thinking upon the matter of contingency because, if you attend to the contingency of man, you must admit the existence of God, but "this question is forbidden socialist man."[21] Lenin was even blunter: "Every religious idea, every idea of a god, even flirting with the idea of god, is unutterable vileness of the most dangerous kind, 'contagion' of the most abominable kind. Millions of sins, filthy deeds, acts of violence, and physical contagions are far less dangerous than the subtle spiritual idea of a god."[22]

Lest any of this sound too abstract, a recent application of this teaching was made in Afghanistan where, after the Communist coup, the loyalty of Afghan officers was tested by the demand that they walk on the *Koran*. Failure to do so was punished by execution.[23]

Creating the New Man

But without God, the status of the world becomes problematic and perilous, to say the least. As Archbishop Sheen once remarked: an atheist is a man with no invisible means of support. Nietzsche and Marx were both aware of this and of the metaphysical requirements for "saving" the world from the great void that opens upon God's "death." They therefore took upon themselves projects to make man exist necessarily; to make his essence, existence; to make him literally god.

This is the metaphysical goal of modern ideology: to remove man from contingency, to end history, to make man completely at home in the world by transforming him into god and his world into paradise through the total transformation of, and total revolution against, reality as it is. Anyone who thinks the goal is less than this—that it is just some kind of social, economic, or even military enterprise— does not understand what is faced in the absence of God or, more accurately, by the willful dismissal of His existence. As Gerhardt Niemeyer has said, "The fact and dynamics of Soviet power cannot be accurately perceived if the underlying nihilism is not grasped."[24]

But how does man become god? How does he change this relationship of his being a caused being, into his being the cause itself? In order to do this modern ideology decided to accept as real only that which man could change. This would enable man to be free and creative in the same way as God. All things then could be contingent in relation to man as they were once thought to be contingent to God. The first step necessary to this undertaking is the denial of what is—the refusal to admit to any limits. As Nietzsche proclaimed, ". . . we have abolished the world of truth," "Nothing is true."[25] Upon the abolition of truth, the two principal means to it—reason and revelation—obviously become irrelevant.

Once truth is removed as an obstacle, all that is required is the acquisition of unlimited power. Modern ideology is the philosophy of unlimited power. Lenin made this explicit in Marxism: "The scientific concept of dictatorship. . . means neither more or less than unlimited power resting directly on force, not limited by anything, not restrained by any laws or any absolute rules, *nothing else but that*."[26] In the *Communist Manifesto*, Marx emphasized that Communists "openly declare that their ends can only be attained by the forceable overthrow of all existing social institutions."[27]

It is important for the appreciation of the nature of today's conflict to understand the primacy of force in Marxism, why force is *required* for revolution. Man is wholly the product of history. Marx says in *The German Ideology* that "the 'inward nature' of men, as well as their 'consciousness' of it, i.e., their 'reason,' has at all times been a historical product."[28] This means man has no nature. For Marx, man is fundamentally determined by the material dialectic as it expresses itself in the economic conditions of class. By definition, people can only act out of their own material self-interest and for no larger purpose. Any purported larger purpose is really just a screen for a class maintaining its economic dominance. Man's reason, then, is just an excresance of this material dialectic, a manifestation of the means of production. Marx asserts that "*intellectual* production changes its character as *material* production is changed."[29] Reason can only know class interests. It is no surprise for Marx to conclude from this that man's mind cannot be changed through reasonable discourse or "by mental criticism. . . but only by the prractical overthrow of the actual social relations"[30] of which man's mind is the determined and inevitable result. So, "not criticism but revolution is the driving force of history. . ."[31] and criticism is only a "weapon" in the battle: "Its object is an *enemy* it wants not to refute but to *destroy*."[32] (So much for what might be hoped for by *reasoning* together with the Soviets.)

As one might imagine, the primacy of force and the denigration of reason totally transmogrify the character of politics. Modern ideology has so changed the character of man that he is no longer a human being. This means concomittantly a change in the way he will be ruled. As a wholly determined, non-rational being, man, of course, can have no free will. Certainly if man is incapable of freely choosing, democracy makes little sense, nor does any constitutional order whose purpose is to leave man free to change himself. Rather the one-party Marxist state becomes the clearly superior vehicle for the forcible, secular transfiguration of the old class man into the classless man. (It should also be noted that this secular salvation is not for the individual man, but placed in the future, as a new idea of mankind to be achieved as a whole.)

The major premise here is that if all the circumstances of man's life can be changed, man himself can be fundamentally changed. Therefore the redemptive state requires total control of the intellectual, moral, economic, social, and physical life of man. (This is why it is called totalitarian.) Bereft of reason and free will, any distinction between man and animal is removed; there is no reason not to rule men as beasts, precisely as the Marxists do. The consent upon which the Marxist state is based is simply an acquiescence of the will to force without reason; it is the consent of a dog to its master.

No longer capable of recognizing men as human beings, Marxists have gone about dehumanizing large portions of mankind according to their pseudo-scientific formula of class, systematically exterminating them as the detritus of history. Those who oppose history have no rights, not even to life. But those who have unlocked history's secret destiny (whether it be the classless society or the thousand-year Reich) have the right to do anything to hasten the work of earthly transfiguration. Lenin enunciated this new ethic: "Everything is moral which is necessary for the annihilation of the old exploiting order."[33] And he showed how it was to be practiced by calling for "purging the Russian land of all kinds of harmful insects."[34]

Beginning under Lenin and up to the present day, some 67 millions of Soviet subjects have been identified as reactionary and harmful insects and eliminated. No one knows how many Chinese in the People's Republic have found themselves in history's way, but the estimates are made in increments of 10 million over a base of 50 million. Hitler, we know, was stopped after 12 million. Most recently we have seen mass slaughter as a means for the total transfiguration of society, employed in Cambodia by the Parisian-trained Marxist Pol Pot. Fellow ideologue Deng Xiaoping in the People's Republic of China expressed (in September of 1980) his approval of Pol Pot, whom the PRC continues to support even though he killed "a relatively large number" of people (a third of his nation), and his admiration for the memory of the Master of the Gulag, Stalin, who was "70 percent" right. According to Truong Nhu Tang, former Minister of Justice for the Viet Cong, there are hundreds of thousands in "re-education camps" in Vietnam. "Literally millions of ordinary citizens were forced to leave their homes and settle in the so called New Economic Zones."[35]. How many have been killed or have died escaping no one knows. Word is finally surfacing of the atrocities committed after the communist coup in Afghanistan in 1978: mass burials alive, drownings in excrements, etc.[36]

All of these things were done by rulers to their subjects. In a communist regime, the relationship between the regime and its subjects is one of war. There is no differentiation in ideology between the reactionary elements within one's society and those without. Both must be eliminated. As long as reality is resistant to its designs, communism will use whatever force is at its disposal to twist reality into conformity with its plan. Since reality is resilient, that state of war is a permanent one. Until the dawning paradise of the classless society, a state of implacable hostility exists.

So the attempted deification of man has backfired into the charnel houses and slave camps of the various Gulags. Those aspiring to be gods have become worse than animals. The great hope of nihilism was that "man will rise higher when he ceases to flow into god." But in God's absence, the distinction dissolves not only between God and man, but also between man and animal. Nicholas Berdyaev said, "Where there is no God, there is no man either."[37] And, as Paul Eidelberg pointed out, "Unless there is a being superior to man, nothing in theory prevents some men from degrading other men to the level of subhuman."[38] Thus emancipated from the oppression of that which was above him—the transcendent—man has found himself under the tyranny of that which was below him. Christopher Dawson warned: "When the prophets are silent and society no longer possesses any channel of communication with the divine world, the way to the lower world is still open and man's frustrated spiritual powers will find their outlet in the unlimited will to power and destruction."

Man, through modern ideology, has tried to make his home here and he has found his home was hell. It is not surprising that the features of this hell/home are similar to those Plato predicted would obtain in any attempt by the state to absorb man totally: the abolition of the private, regimentation, the destruction of the family, etc.

But it is obviously not enough to say that this is despotic, tyrannical rule, that it is ruling men as if they were beasts. The boundless passions of old-fashioned tyranny are familiar enough in the modern version of Idi Amin et al. The old-fashioned tyranny is not ordered to anything but the boundless passion of the tyrant's will. His regime resides in his person; it seldom survives the tyrant's own existence; it is not systemic. Ideology, by contrast, institutionalizes its total inversion of reality in an official system based upon a comprehensive, if perverted, explanation of life's meaning. We are confronted with, as Gerhart Niemeyer has said, "the logically structured public institution of evil."[39] Niemeyer states, "In other words, we are today facing evil that issues not so much from passions and misdirected loves as rather from semi-rational idea systems and government planning. . . Evil in this century has come dressed in the mantle of apparent reason, the logic of history or the superman, or both, an ideology set up on the throne of public philosophy and enlisting the conscience in the planned pattern of logical murder."[40] This unprecedented nature is expressed, as Albert Camus pointed out, in such things as "slave camps under the flag of freedom, massacres justified by philanthropy."[41]

Things Worth Fighting For

Pius XII proclaimed in his Christmas message of 1950, "Never has history known a more gigantic disorder."[42] Father Murray commented, "The uniqueness of the disorder resides, I take it, in the unparalleled depth of its vertical dimension; it goes to the very roots of order and disorder in the world—the nature of man, his destiny, and the meaning of human history."[43]

Therefore, as one would expect, the conflict between communism and reality is engaged at every level of existence: social, cultural, economic, physical, spiritual. It is implacable and unremitting. It will only be over with the total triumph of the world proletarian revolution and the metaphysical reconstruction of man. Internal oppression and external aggression are the inseparable means for this task.[44]

War will be used according to its prospects of success. As Father Murray said, "It is all a matter of the measure of risk that war would entail and of the measure of its usefulness for the World Revolution."[45] "To the Communist war . . . is strictly and coldly a means to an end. And the end is strictly defined."[46] The existence of nuclear weapons in no way changes this understanding. This is very clear in the Soviet literature. "The correlation of war and politics is fully valid under conditions where weapons of mass destruction are applied."[47] "Armed struggle with the use of nuclear missiles and other weapons will ultimately be subordinated to the interests of definite policy, it will become a means of attaining definite political aims."[48]

The Marxist analysis of the peace movement in the West is also very interesting and instructive: "[Contemporary 'social pacifists'] proceed from the position that the threat of nuclear war has made armed struggle for political purposes impossible."[49] The Marxist mind must identify such a proposition as a ruse, since it is by definition impossible for anyone in the imperialist, bourgeois world to advance anything but his own interests. So they conclude that "the threat of nuclear war has become for them a means for justifying a policy of the preservation of the capitalist order on earth, and an instrument for intimidating the world liberation movement and to achieve the spiritual disarmament of anti-Imperialist forces."[50] The existence of nuclear weapons does not modify Lenin's teaching that "disarmament is tantamount to complete abandonment of the class struggle point of view, to renunciation of all thought of revolution."[51]

Therefore, "to put 'disarmament' in the (Socialist) programme is tantamount to making the general declaration: 'We are opposed to the use of arms.' There is as little Marxism in this as there would be if we were to say: 'We are opposed to violence.' "[52] It would be utterly absurd for a Marxist to believe that a weapon by its very nature could fundamentally modify his ideology or in some way exist above or beyond ideology. As we know, by definition, violence is the theoretically correct resolution to the class conflict. It simply must be engaged in at a level that does not imperil the Revolution itself.

The whole assumption behind the Christian "just war" tradition is that there is a shared common good which transcends war and therefore limits it, no matter how grievous the disputes between the combatants. But to suppose, in negotiating with the communists, that this moral universe is shared, that they are seized by some sudden apprehension of the common humanity of all men, is a grievous error. They may eschew total nuclear war, not because the elimination of all civilized life is evil, but for strategic reasons— because the revolution itself may be destroyed, and history cannot permit this: the end of the temporal world is the ideologue's *summum malum*.

What, then, is at stake in this conflict? Everything. What is the nature of the conflict? It is spiritual and metaphysical, it imperils the highest moral values of man. It is a struggle over who man is. It therefore is ultimately a struggle over God. It is a crisis between us and within us. The conflict between us is not between the people and cultures of the East and West, but between the totalitarian regime which makes war upon its own people, and against all who are unlike it. It demands the homogenization of the world for its justification. Anyone who thinks that the ambitions of the Soviet Union are less than global must explain what common enterprise could possibly bring together the PLO, East Germans, Vietnamese, North Koreans, Bulgarians, and Cubans in Nicaragua.[53] But the underlying spiritual crisis is not so clearly delineated between them and us.

As Solzhenitsyn writes, "The battle is not between them and you, but between you and yourselves."[54] What does he mean? He alludes to the extent to which we do not realize that the conflict is spiritual: we are blind and will be incapable of recovery. No new basing mode for the MX missile or high frontier technology will save us from the collision this blindness will cause. It is those who do not see the spiritual nature of the conflict who tell us that, in fact, there *is* no real conflict, that the Cold War is a psychiatric problem, that with patience the commercial materialism of the West and the ideological materialism of the East will peacefully converge.

There are two reasons for the failure to admit to the existence of the moral horrors that have been and still are at the heart of the 20th century. One is moral cowardice: the desire not to know, a willful ignorance that attempts to absolve one from any exertions in respect to these horrors. The other is complicity. "This split in the world," Solzhenitsyn warned, "is less terrifying than the similarity of the disease afflicting its main sections."[55] We mean complicity in the sense that the same materialistic assumptions about man's nature are fundamentally shared with our ideological opponents, along with the notion that they are morally superior and "on the right side of history." Some, such as Andrew Young, say explicitly that "It may take the destruction of Western civilization to allow the rest of the world to emerge as a free and brotherly society." Others, greater in number, subscribe to a secularized humanism in which, as Solzhenitsyn said, "Man—the master of the world—does not bear any evil within himself, and all the defects of life are caused by misguided social systems which must therefore be corrected."[56] There is no "task higher than the attainment of happiness on earth."[57] Unwilling to recognize evil in ourselves we become incapable of recognizing its existence elsewhere. We become possessed by a pathological good will founded in a combination of a pragmatism that refuses to take ideas seriously and a resurrected Pelagianism that refuses to admit to the existence of sin. We end up unable to take seriously or even to believe in the threat to our own existence. Surely we are all good people at heart, we think; surely no one can take seriously these ideas about violently restructuring existence.

A Test of Will

This is the moral blindness that emanates from what Solzhenitsyn calls "an autonomous, irreligious, humanistic consciousness." The disease has infected the West by eroding the very basis for the assertion of our common humanity just as it has already been eroded in the East through Marxism. (The dehumanization of the unborn comes to mind as an example. The U.S. Supreme Court admitted, in *Roe v. Wade*, that it could not distinguish between the human and the non-human.) We are told, by modern science, that there is no principle of order in the universe, just random repetition; by psychiatry, that thought is physiological and basically irrational; by modern philosophy, that external reality is not accessible to our minds. Hans Reichenbach asserts in *The Rise of Scientific Philosophy* that "We have no absolutely conclusive evidence that there is a physical world and we have no absolutely conclusive evidence either that we exist."[58]

What would one be willing to die to defend, based on this view of the world? This kind of skepticism leads to the logical subjectification of all values, the reduction of good and evil to individual preferences that have no defense outside of themselves, but which need no defense since there are no external objective criteria by which to judge their moral worth. If there are no pre-existing, intelligible ends toward which man is ordered by nature, every individual must invent, in an arbitrary and subjective manner, some ends by which to guide his actions and order his life. Since no common good can be known, each individual is free to make up his own "good." The way one lives then becomes a matter of "lifestyle." The elevation of the words "lifestyle" to their present prominence is an indication of the total loss of any serious meaning in one's choice of how to live. What once was man's most profound ethical concern has been reduced to an element of fashion.

This trivialization of life is reflected in the substitution of behaviorism for the study of ethics in school curriculum. One may no longer speak of virtue, for who is to say what is good and just? The consideration of what man "ought" to do is therefore demoted to a study of what he does. Man is seen as a bundle of nerve endings subject to the manipulations of his environment. If you wish to change him, change the stimuli to which he is exposed. This is the premise from which our social planners and sex clinics all operate. The road to happiness is in the next housing project or orgasm.

This same perspective reduces the larger claims of democratic government to the study of: who gets what, where, when, and how? There being no common good, everything can be understood in terms of self-interest. The high sounding words of the *Declaration of Independence* and *Constitution* are just a cloak for the self-aggrandizement of individuals who benefit most from the "system." In fact, this school of thought teaches us that all "systems" can be understood in these same terms—the Soviet Union's as well as our own. We can point to different means of distribution in each, but are left powerless to make any fundamental moral distinctions between the two.

As an American investment banker recently opined in respect to the Soviet-style regime in Poland, "Who knows what political system works? The only test that we care about is: can they pay their bills?"[59] This implied equality of regimes leads us to believe that the Soviet Union calculates its self-interest in the same way as we do. This has resulted in huge miscalculations on our part concerning Soviet behavior and intentions which now directly endanger the freedom of the West.

Moral subjectivism, as C.S. Lewis warned, "must be the destruction of the society which accepts it." By denying objective truth and morality, moral subjectivism undermines democracy in the worst way. It not only neglects the cultivation of virtue in the young, but, worse still, tells them there is no such thing as virtue. Thus it is doubly culpable for eroding both the practical and theoretical foundations of free government. With each person a law unto himself, free political community becomes impossible. Anarchy logically follows, as does its swift substitution by tyranny. People have always shown their preference for despotism over disorder.

It is fair to say that with this loss of reality comes loss of purpose. And when people do not understand the purpose for which they live, they find it difficult to exert the effort necessary to keep alive. (I recently heard a radio advertisement encouraging people to breathe—sponsored, ironically enough, by a religious institution.) People simply will not make the sacrifices necessary to exercise power unless they understand that that power serves a good end. If we are taught that we cannot distinguish between ends, or that knowledge of a good end is unavailable, the evisceration of our will logically follows. Once purpose is gone, we can expect to do whatever seems easiest and most gratifying at any given time. This is the attitude Solzhenitsyn said he had perceived in the United States and the West: "Go ahead, give it up. . . Just let us live in peace and quiet. . . Just let us play tennis and golf in peace and quiet; just let us mix our cocktails in peace and quiet as we are accustomed to doing; just let us see the beautiful toothy smile with a glass in hand on every advertisement page of our magazines."[60] Anyone who thinks Solzhenitsyn is overdramatizing the moral infantilization of the West has only to spend an hour or two before the television to have his worst fears confirmed.

The moral disarmament of the United States has resulted in a political and strategic retreat that is familiar enough to anyone who has cared to compare a map of the world now to one of 35 years ago. To the extent the United States has lost the belief in the moral legitimacy of its purpose, it has retreated from the world. And the retreat has been precipitous. Edward Luttwak warns, "Not to stand and assert the truth in the war of ideas means to suffer delegitimization now, and then the eventual defeat in the practical realms of policy and strategy."[61] This is precisely the sequence that things have been following, and will continue to follow unless Western statesmen undertake their moral obligation to tell the truth.

All of this may be so abstract as to remove it from the realm of daily experience in the West. How can this ideology really be what the communists intend? Certainly in the world of diplomats, among whom I move according to my current profession, an embarassing mention of this problem is seldom made. But it is the duty of political leaders, whose job it is to protect us, to tell us the truth. More especially, the leaders of the Church have this same duty—because there is no greater enemy of the Kingdom of Heaven than the Kingdom of the Earth.

"Evil that is a public design and murders without a troubled conscience," says Niemeyer, "imposes on statesmen as well as private citizens the obligation to take a stand."[62] Niemeyer emphasizes what is at stake in doing so: "To turn one's back on the evidence of a particularly dangerous evil gives one the appearance of willingness to consort with it which amounts to a betrayal of the very foundations on which government rests."[63] Opposing it, on the other hand, can reinforce those very foundations and preserve them. This is why Solzhenitsyn says: "Whenever you help the person persecuted in the Soviet Union, you not only display magnanimity and nobility, you're defending not only them but yourselves as well. You're defending your own future."[64]

Once an evil is recognized, one is morally obligated to oppose it, to take upon oneself the sacrifices necessary for its ultimate extinction. This obligation does not translate into an insane holy war which might well create a greater evil than it set out to cure, but, within the limits of prudence, it should set the direction of one's actions. Does this mean nuclear war? Did Solzhenitsyn have nuclear weapons? No, he simply had the enormous spiritual courage to tell the truth, which the Soviet regime recognizes as its greatest enemy. It fears truth far more than radiation.

To combat the false view of man communism offers, we must recover the spiritual fullness of our own. Ironically, this very struggle may lead us to recovery, to the spiritual blaze Solzhenitsyn demands of us. Whittaker Chambers gave the hope that, "For the West, the struggle is its own solution. Out of the struggle itself, the West may rediscover in itself, or otherwise develop, forces that can justify its survival."

That survival is threatened now by the same disease in two forms, two kinds of nihilism: one with intestines and one without. Either one can kill us. One is nihilism bent through destruction to build the brave new world; the other is the nihilism of the death wish, of moral extinction, of peace in the nothingness that follows when all is given up to survive. Both go hand in hand, for only together can they bring us *Pax Sovietica*.

Can we learn from the sufferings of others, asks Solzhenistyn. This is an enormous question, on whose answer a great deal ultimately relies, for it leads us finally to ask: can we learn from the sufferings of Christ? In fact, we are asked as Christians to join in Christ's sufferings, from which we not only learn but earn our eternal salvation. Could it be that we are asked to join in the sufferings of those oppressed as well? And what is it we are to learn from those sufferings? The profoundest truth about man—that those sufferings prepare us for and serve (however mysteriously they will be transformed) the coming of the Kingdom of Heaven. That through suffering is the resolution of the war within us of which St. James spoke. That there is no resolution to the war within us without suffering. That the only real iron curtain runs through the soul of each one of us.[65] And we must understand that this is where the battle is being fought before we can realize the nature of today's conflict, and of what is at stake in the true peace of Christ's cross.

NOTES

1. John Courtney Murray, S.J., *We Hold These Truths* (New York: Sherd and Ward, 1960), p. 252.

2. Patrick Glynn, "Nuclear Polemics," *Journal of Contemporary Studies*, Summer 1982, p. 62.

3. Aleksandr I. Solzhenitsyn, "Solzhenitsyn: The Voice of Freedom," (AFL-CIO, Publication No. 152), p. 30.

4. Robert A. Goldwin (ed.), *America Armed* (Chicago: Rand McNally and Co., 1963) p. 86.

5. *Ibid.*

6. Aleksandr Solzhenitsyn, "A Soviet Martyr's Anguished Plea," *The Wall Street Journal*, September 19, 1973.

7. Murray, *op. cit.*, p. 261.

8. *Ibid.*

9. As cited in *Ibid.*, p. 259.

10. Goldwin, *op. cit.*, p. 83.

11. Aleksandr Solzhenitsyn, "A World Split Apart," *Vital Speeches of the Day*, September 1, 1978, p. 683.

12. Jean-Jacques Rousseau, *The Reveries of a Solitary Walker* (New York: Burt Franklin, 1971), p. 114.

13. As cited in Paul Eidelberg, *Beyond Detente* (La Salle: Sherwood Sugden, 1977), p. 74.

14. Friedrich Nietzsche, *The Will to Power*.

15. See Martin Heidegger, *Introduction to Metaphysics*.

16. M.C. D'Arcy, S.J., *The Meaning and Matter of History* (New York: The Noonday Press, 1967), p. 165.

17. Friedrich Nietzsche, *Beyond Good and Evil.*

18. As cited in Henri de Lubac, S.J., *The Drama of Atheist Humanism* (New York: Meridien Books, 1963), p. 17.

19. *Ibid.*, p. 72.

20. V.I. Lenin, "Defeat of One's Own Government in Imperialist War," 1915, *Selected Works* (New York: International Publishers), vol. 5, p. 147.

21. Karl Marx, *Writings of the Young Marx on Philosophy and Society* (New York: Anchor Books, Doubleday and Company, Inc., 1967), pp. 65-66.

22. V.I. Lenin, "Letter from Lenin to A.M. Gorky," 1913, *Selected Works,* (New York: International Publishers), vol. 11, pp. 675-676.

23. Michael Barry, "Afghanistan—Another Cambodia?", *Commentary* August 1982, p. 34.

24. Gerhart Niemeyer, "Foreign Policy and Morality: A Contemporary Perspective," Intercollegiate Review Reprint from *The Intercollegiate Review* Spring 1980, p. 6.

25. As cited in de Lubac, *op. cit.*, p. 29.

26. As cited in Eidelberg, *op. cit.*, p. 75.

27. *Ibid.*, p. 104.

28. *Ibid.*, pp. 65-66.

29. *Ibid.*, p. 65.

30. *Ibid.*, p. 67.

31. *Ibid.*

32. *Ibid.*

33. *Ibid.*, p. 70.

34. *Ibid.*

35. Truong Nhu Tang, "The 'Liberation' of Vietnam," *The Washington Post*, October 7, 1982, p. A27.

36. Barry, *op. cit.*

37. As cited in de Lubac, *op. cit.*, p. 31.

38. Eidelberg, *op. cit.*

39. Niemeyer, *op. cit.*, p. 3.

40. *Ibid.*, p. 2.

41. As cited in *Ibid.*

42. As cited in Murray, *op. cit.*, p. 253.

43. *Ibid.*

44. Vladimir Bukovsky, "The Peace Movement and the Soviet Union," *Commentary*, May 1982, p. 39.

45. Murray, *op. cit.*

46. *Ibid.*, p. 80.

47. Colonel S. Tyushkevich, *Communist of the Armed Forces*, November 1975.

48. Colonel B. Byely, Colonel Y. Ozyuba, and Colonel G. Fyodorev et al., *Marxism-Leninism on War and the Army*, Progress Publishers, Moscow, 1973.

49. Major-General A.S. Milovidev, *The Philosophical Heritage of V.I. Lenin and the Problems of Contemporary War*, Editor-in-Chief Voyenizdat, Moscow, 1972, p. 53.

50. *Ibid.*

51. V.I. Lenin, *Collected Works*, Progress Publishers, Moscow, vol. 23, p. 59.

52. *Ibid.*

53. Sol W. Sanders, "International Outlook," *Business Week*, September 13, 1982, p. 48.

54. Aleksandr Solzhenitsyn, "Solzhenitsyn in Zurich: An Interview," *Encounter*, April 1976, p. 14.

55. Aleksandr Solzhenitsyn, "A World Split Apart," p. 683.

56. *Ibid.*, p. 680.

57. *Ibid.*, p. 683.

58. As cited in D'Arcy, *op. cit.*, p. 19.

59. As cited in John Lofton, "John Lofton's Journal," *Washington Times*, September 29, 1982.

60. Solzhenitsyn, "Solzhenitsyn: The Voice of Freedom," p. 12.

61. Edward Luttwak, "How to Think About Nuclear War," *Commentary*, August 1982, p. 28

62. Niemeyer, *op. cit.*, p. 3.

63. *Ibid.*, p. 7.

64. Solzhenitsyn, "Solzhenitsyn: The Voice of Freedom," p. 24.

65. I am indebted to Christopher Derrick for this thought.

Intellectual Origins of the Peace Movement

Rev. James V. Schall, S.J.

The illusion of a country in which intellectuals dictate is very old and goes back to Plato. The intellectuals want to impose their philosophy on average people who don't want philosophy. They want to eat, to make money, to make love, and to get on with life. But thinkers would transform these people into angels dedicated to pure intellect. This is behind the desire to transform the world, and it is a very dangerous illusion. Intellectuals in Marxist states do not rule; they are instruments of petty and vicious politicians.

> —Czeslaw Milosz, "Interview with Nobel Laureate,"
> *National Catholic Register*, June 13, 1982.

I can imagine no man will look with more horror on the End than the conscientious revolutionary who has, in a sense sincerely, been justifying cruelties and injustices inflicted on millions of his contemporaries by the benefits which he hopes to confer on future generations: generations who, as one terrible moment now reveals to him, were never going to exist.

> —C.S. Lewis, *The World's Last Night and Other Essays*,
> New York: Macmillan, 1960, p. 111.

The Meanings of Peace

The rhetoric of peace is paradoxical. Neville Chamberlain's confident hopes for "peace in our time" after the Munich Conference in 1938, along with the results of the Versailles Treaty of 1919, have become classical examples of how "peace" pacts can lead to war or injustice.[1] Yet, how much worse it might have been, we reflect, had that war, World War II, been lost—had a Hitler been able to conquer Europe, as well he might have. Had German scientists invented the A-Bomb first, followed by the Luftwaffe dropping it on, say, Liverpool, would we have had the same sort of anguish that we seem to have now about Hiroshima? Or would we have blamed ourselves for not inventing it first? Or would we have rejoiced on our "morality" under such a tyranny? Wars not fought, of course, do not necessarily mean that "peace" is operative. Peace is the "tranquility of order," as Augustine defined it, Augustine from whom we have perhaps turned away too much if we would think clearly on the actual conditions of any realistic or realizable peace.[2] Political philosophers describe a sort of perfect "order" in the worst regimes. Aristotle even gave us a sort of handbook about how to set one up and keep it (1314b ff.). The modern concentration camp or Gulag is indeed quite well "ordered" to its grizzly end. Slavery in the ancient world was the alternative to death, the just result of losing a war. But the ancients were not at all sure which was worse.

Thus, "peace" must not be merely "order," but justice also. Justice, however, as it turns out, is harsh, the cruelest of the practical virtues. Those who live under its strict regimen poignantly feel its symbolic blindness. Aristotle found that revolutions were almost always caused by diverging perceptions of justice: those equal in some things thinking they were equal in all, those unequal in some things holding they were unequally superior in other areas (1310a19 ff.). The philosophic tradition understood the idea of "concord," the notion that a certain relational harmony existed in a polity when everything was in its proper place. Yet, this same tradition did not think that such concord could happen very often—perhaps never in foreign affairs, as Thucydides intimated—so there arose considerable question about whether the politician responsible for order could ever be a philosopher responsible for the truth. Indeed, Augustine would simply suggest that this longed-for union of politics and philosophy could not exist in this world, so that the kind of "peace" we could expect would be based largely on force and inequality, though, even on this hypothesis, there would be a wide variation. To propose "peace" as precisely a *political* goal was perhaps the most dangerous illusion, since it could easily result in the betrayal of truth in the name of merely external order. A utopian doctrine, however valuable as an analytical tool, could not in itself allow for the pragmatic arrangements that might, at best, be expected for a tolerable human life.

All through our history, there is a sense in which the abstract ideal of a perfectly peaceful world somehow became the intellectual arm of tyranny—no one spoke of this issue more eloquently than Burke—while the acceptance of a fair degree of political imperfection became the only basis for a tolerable civil life, for a "peace" in this world. Aquinas put it so well: "Human law is directed to the multitude of men, among whom the greater part are not perfect. Thus, human law does not prohibit all vices from which the virtuous abstain, but only those grave ones, from which it is possible for the great majority of men to abstain. . . ." (I-II, 96, 2).

There is found an amusing passage in Boswell that might be of some instruction here:

> A literary lady of large fortune was mentioned, as one who did good to many, but by no means by stealth (ie, in private), and instead of "blushing to find it fame," acted evidently from vanity. JOHNSON: "I have seen no beings who do as much good from benevolence, as she does from whatever motive. . . . No, Sir, to act from pure benevolence is not possible for finite human beings. Human benevolence is mingled with vanity, interest, or some other motives."

Boswell recounted these reflections in 1776, almost exactly when our own political ancestors were beginning to ponder how to establish a republic based upon the same view of man, a being in whom there is both sin and fallibility. And too, these were very Augustinian words, reminders of the dangers of not accounting for human beings as they actually are. In the contemporary discussions of war, we can, at best, hope for a "probable peace"—more than "hope" or "probability" was never justly promised to us. But we can only hope for this on the condition that we are willing to understand very clearly what we are up against—that we are prepared to acknowledge the existence of motives, organizations, and ambitions that do not arise primarily from benevolence. We can make some progress only if we do not try to change completely the kind of "finite human beings" we are, if we do not attempt to transform ourselves "into angels dedicated to pure intellect," who are surprised on the Last Day to discover that the "order" of the world they proposed for "peace" would never come to pass. There is in much of this utopianism a sort of hidden hatred for the kind of creation, and particularly the hand of redemption, that we have in fact been given.

Peace in Religious Tradition

These initial remarks about justice and fallenness are, perhaps, why we find our most frequent and poignant descriptions of "peace," not in the philosophers, but in revelation. The inscription on the walls of Monte Casino in Italy, the first Benedictine Abbey, even after it was rebuilt following its destruction by bombing during World War II, was *PAX:* peace. And it was noteworthy that the "peace" found in its walls was something that could continue whether in war or peace. In Scripture, peace was described as a gift of God, radically depending on something more profound than justice.[3] Creation was rooted primarily in mercy, not justice, a doctrine of Aquinas that is of monumental significance (I, 21, 4; *CG*, II, 28). Indeed, it seems precisely this priority of mercy to justice that lies at the heart of the difficulties intrinsic to modern "peace" thinking, since there seems to be a subtle effort to achieve political peace by human efforts alone. Human efforts are not to be abandoned, of course, but they can easily be erected into their own autonomous, closed worldview which allows for nothing but what is under man's power.

Peace in Aquinas was always considered to be the *effect* of charity or mercy, whereas concord was the effect of justice in the classical tradition and therefore not easily achieved. The main reason why modern "peace" efforts are not entirely successful is because they claim to be products of man's autonomous intelligence[4]. There seems to be a connection, in this sense, between ideology and revelation that cannot be ignored, since the "peace" programs of the ideologies are offered as substitutes for the "peace" proposed in revelation: how it comes about, how it is to be achieved. During most of the modern era, revelation and ideology were considered to be, indeed considered *themselves* to be, hostile to one another. What is new in the current context, at least from the point of view of ideology, seems to be the possibility of enlisting religion in the service of modern absolutist movements under the aegis of "peace" conceived as the avoidance of nuclear war. The ramifications of how all of this sorts itself out will be, in part, the burden of these reflections on the intellectual origins of the "peace" movement.

The manner in which Aquinas dealt with "peace," then, is of great significance here since he rarely talked simply of "peace," but rather of *"vera pax"* and *"falsa pax,"* as if to acknowledge the ease with which one can be taken for the other in actual circumstances. He wrote:

> True peace cannot be had except through a desire of the true good, because all evil, although it appears under some form of the good, whence it satisfies our appetites in part, has many defects about which the appetites remain disturbed and restless. Whence, the true good cannot be except in the good and about good things. Peace, however, which is of evil things, is an apparent, not true peace. (II-II, 29, 2, ad 3)

Peace, in other words, is primarily brought about through knowing the truth about good things and the spiritual ways these are achieved. The possibility, and even likelihood, of a "false" peace, therefore, which leaves us "disturbed and restless," however lofty the rhetoric, is something that should be consciously present in all discussions of peace, in all political efforts to bring it about.

Thus, in the Gospel of John, we read of a "peace that the world cannot give" (14:27). Clearly, such peace is not merely the erection of a perfect political regime by civil methods. This peace "that the world cannot give" seems present in all sorts of regimes—seems not to be directed primarily at the political as such. There are truly holy people, in other words, in every sort of regime. Contrariwise, the "peace" the world "can" give is, obviously, not that which it *cannot* give. And Satan's kingdom was said not be divided against itself (Mat., 12:26). There was evidently an "order" to it. The notion of a peace that the world cannot give again comes into Aquinas' principle that creation is gratuitous, not dependent on anything in the world itself but rather on the "reasons" of revelation and those contained in the natural order (I-II, 91, 4).

In Ezechiel, moreover, we find something more ominous: "I am going to stretch my hand over the prophets who have empty visions and give lying predictions; they will not be admitted to the council of my people. . . . You will learn that I am the Lord Yahweh, since they have misled my people by saying 'Peace' when there is no peace" (14:9). False prophets preach precisely "peace," whereas true prophets can tell when "peace" is its opposite—"Peace, peace, but there is no peace," Jeremiah had also cried (6:14). We cannot avoid the impression that, especially in Scripture, we are warned about the ambiguities to which the cries for "peace" are open. We know the closer we get to holiness, the more likely we are to be deceived, the more likely we are to call our ways God's ways. We can suspect that this danger, so obvious at a personal level, is even more subtle at the level of nations and powers.

Pope John XXIII's famous Encyclical, *Pacem in Terris*, (1963) began with these words: "Peace on earth, which men of every era so eagerly yearned for, can be established only if the order laid down by God be dutifully observed." These very words, of course, suggest not merely that there is a "right" order in the universe, but also that there is an "order" *not* laid down by God—that is, there is a possibility of man's choosing against the good, and this is allowed in God's providence. This suggests, then, that not every path actually leads to true peace. There is a real drama in history, with things really at stake. Indeed, this suggests that the real reason we may miss true peace is that this false order is presented to us under the guise of true peace. This is strengthened by the very title of this Encyclical, "Peace on Earth," (*pacem in terris*), a title which seems to come from a passage in Luke, one not cited in the document itself, but one which gives much pause about any overly sanguine notion about "peace on earth." " 'Do you supose I am here to bring peace on earth (*pacem in terram*)?' Jesus asked. 'No, I tell you, but rather division (*separationem*)' " (12:51). The struggles between true and false peace are thus themselves rooted in something in a sense higher than the mere peace of external order, which can be contrary to the truth. This more sober notion of "peace" in our philosophical and theological traditions—how it is achieved, what is opposed to it—is something we ignore at our peril. There is something higher than "peace" at any cost. "Division" or "separation" is better than false peace. This is why, in Aquinas, peace is always a *consequence*, not a direct object of our strivings, a result of truth and mercy and charity.

Peace, then, is ever a result, not a cause. If we are to seek peace, we must seek something besides peace. As a gift of God, it can only be achieved by the ways of God which were set down by Him. "My ways," not "your ways," as it was described in the Old Testament. The question ever arises, then, whether we can expect "justice" without first addressing ourselves to questions arising out of revelation. While Plato could ponder whether we could even talk of full virtue without considering the perfect polis, revelation began in any sort of polis and continues in any sort of community. Its presence does not first depend upon a "rearrangement" of political or economic structures; it does not define its task in those terms. Rather it commands a change of heart (Mk., 1:15). Spiritual motivations and objectives are required. To seek any other sort of "peace" seems to be rather presumptuous: an effort to create an order in the world dependent upon man's decision about the form and content of a "peaceful" world, a decision that displaces effectively the "end" of man as found in revelation.

Scripture, of course, does not teach a sort of "quietism" in this regard. Grace does not deprive men of authentic human action, but it does warn about theories of "peace" which are finally and formally derived from the autonomous human intellect, from a concept of the "necessary forces of history" outside divine guidance (Rom., 2:21-24; 1 Cor., 1, 17-25). This is why there is a component of obedience, reasoned obedience, in all faith and morality, precisely because what causes peace does not derive primarily or ultimately from ourselves, even though when it comes to us, it remains properly ours. Granted this, Paul can tell the Romans, "Do all you can to live at peace with everyone" (12:18). "The Lord of Peace" (2 Thess., 3:14) restored "peace through the Cross" (Eph., 2:10). This is not, be it again noted, primarily a "political" action, despite the fact that Christ, like Socrates, was executed by the state. It is the Spirit, then, that "brings peace" (Gal., 5:22). "The good news of peace is brought by Jesus" (Acts, 10:36). The religious side of "peacemaking," thus, ought not to be confused with political efforts to prevent war or violence. Both have their proper places. Indeed, there is a sense in which we can wonder about the necessity of both.

Peace and Tyranny

Peace, we are frequently reminded, is not, then, merely the "absence of war or hostilities," since any successful tyranny prevents "war" and usually "violence." Hobbes, indeed, seems to have posited "peace" upon the denial of any specific content to human nature in reason or revelation. He used absolute force to remove religion or philosophy from the public order. The primacy of survival, particularly the survival of the "race" as we see it in current discussions, seems often closer to Hobbes than to a religion based on the notion of personal eternal life. Indeed, the continued life of "man" on earth—an abstraction down the ages—seems perilously near to substituting itself for the classical teachings about immortality and personal resurrection. From this arises a theoretical method to reabsorb the individual into the collectivity.[5] Further, the principle of survival at any cost, of security as such, seems one of the main justifications for a sort of voluntary entrance into actual tyranny in which nothing is worth opposition except physical death, particularly death of the species. The complete absence of war might thus be considered philosophically as the intellectual victory of tyranny in one basic sense. This would be complete not merely in the sense that the "tyrant" (of whatever type) took over, but in the sense that he does so with the people "willing" to allow or even encourage him to do so. In order to be "moral," the people chose a completely immoral order as the most reasonable choice.

The principal project or task of the modern successful tyrant, then, is not the *use* of force, but rather the erection of an *argument* about force which convinces those against whom it *might* be used to accept the tyranny freely and, as it were, "morally." Aristotle seemed to think this might be possible; certainly the Soviet dissidents do.[6] And this "victory of tyranny," chosen as an act of "virtue," must be based on a theory which denies metaphysical freedom and the common nature of the people, of the human being. That is, it must be based on a theory in which there is no "structure" or abiding "nature" in man. The argument for "surrender" in this sense represents also the philosophical destruction of Western intelligence.

Professor Leo Strauss, in his famous essay on tyranny, wrote in this regard:

> The classics thought that, owing to the weakness or dependence of human nature, universal happiness is impossible and therefore they did not dream of a fulfillment of History and hence not a meaning of History. They saw with their mind's eye a society within which that

happiness of which human nature is capable would be possible in the highest degree: that society is the best regime. But because they saw how limited man's power is, they held that the actualization of the best regime depends on chance. Modern man, dissatisfied with utopias and scorning them, has tried to find a guarantee for the actualization of the best social order. In order to succeed, or rather in order to be able to believe that he could succeed, he had to lower the goal of man. One form in which this was done was to replace moral virtue by universal recognition, or to replace happiness by the satisfaction deriving from universal recognition. The classical solution is utopian in the sense that its actualization is improbable. The modern solution is utopian in the sense that its actualization is impossible. The classical solution supplies a stable standard by which to judge of any actual order. The modern solution eventually destroys the very idea of a standard that is independent of actual solutions.[7]

For Strauss, the final form of tyranny on earth would be precisely the capacity of the state to determine the content and structure of nature, man, and society. "From the Universal Tyrant, however," he went on,

> There is no escape. Thanks to the conquest of nature and to the completely unabashed substitution of suspicion and terror for law, the Universal and Final Tyrant has at his disposal practically unlimited means for ferreting out, and for extinguishing, the most modest efforts in the direction of thought.... The coming of the universal and homogenous state will be the end of philosophy on earth.[8]

These latter remarks suggest why the contemporary analysis of "war" must be seen in the light of theoretical descriptions of what happens when relevant distinctions about human worth are subsumed into a single standard of "avoiding war" or achieving "absolute security." To what degree the "peace" movement is itself a function of the effort to establish just this sort of tyranny is a question too few are willing to ask, although it lies at the heart of the practical problem.[9]

The question of weapons and their use, then, is *not* the crucial issue. Rather it is the *political* manipulation of the weapons threat as an argument to change regimes *without* the need to use such weapons. The issue in question is one of intelligence and nerves, of perception about what is the nature of the civil order and its own good. Hannah Arendt put it with her usual trenchant force:

> It is as though the nuclear armament race has turned into some sort of tentative warfare in which the opponents demonstrate to each other the destructiveness of the weapons in their possession; and while it is always possible that this deadly game of ifs and whens may suddenly turn into the real thing, it is by no means inconceivable that one day victory and defeat may end a war that never exploded into reality....

Seventeen years after Hiroshima, our technical mastery of the means of destruction is fast approaching the point where all non-technical factors in warfare, such as troop morale, strategy, general competence and even sheer chance, are completely eliminated so that results can be calculated with perfect precision in advance. Once this point is reached, the results of mere tests and demonstrations could be as conclusive evidence to the experts for victory or defeat as the battlefield, the conquest of territory, the breakdown of communications, et cetera, have formerly been to the military experts on either side.[10]

Alexander Solzhenitsyn has, in his own way, also stressed the force of this kind of approach, one that suggests that the problems are *political* rather than materialist calculations of what "might" happen if nuclear weapons are used in certain places or ways.[11] Jean-Francois Deniau, the French diplomat, writes in the same fashion: "It is not a question of unleashing global war, and we can think that no one desires a global war. The problem is precisely to respond to a Soviet strategy which is, as far as possible, and in as much as possible, *to win without war*".[12]

Peace as a Political Weapon

In this context, therefore, it is very curious that marxist sources are beginning to supply analyses of Christian thinking on the war question, which are explicitly based on the "peace" or anti-nuclear movements as a sort of raw material for Soviet strategy. Under the cover of anti-war and anti-weapons sentiments, evidently noble and worthwhile goals, we are beginning to see in marxist sources efforts to use this movement to bring religious structures especially into a force for achieving classical marxist-socialist goals. From a conservative side, Professor Thomas Molnar has already suggested some of this, so it is doubly interesting to see the same sort of analysis appearing almost simultaneously in marxist journals.[13]

Carl Marzani, writing in *Monthly Review*, asked rhetorically whether the Vatican can be an ally of the Left? Granting that the Holy Father is a so-called "conservative" on what are called "moral" or "social" matters like family life, abortion, and personal sanctity (not very important items with a whole world to reconstruct, to be sure), Marzani sought to enlist the Pope's influence for the same goals as the marxist worldview. Rarely in the past has Christian argumentation seemed open to such an interpretation. When it does, we can legitimately wonder who has changed: the marxists or certain Christians? What is of special interest to us here is Marzani's conclusion, which again intimates that the real issue is a certain subtle strategy about how to make political progress *without* war, whatever forces or weapons we might have in the silos or magazines. This was Deniau's point. The real issue in the context of our times is whether the fear of war can be used to achieve political gain. Marzani wrote:

> One final, and personal, word, from a thoroughbred atheist. There is an unspoken feeling among many progressives that the Catholic Church is a more backward, a more superstitious, religion, than Protestant or Jewish varieties. I have always felt, with Graham Greene, that if one could swallow God, the Immaculate Conception should prove a minor problem. There are differences among the religious and the non-religious on social issues, but *in the face of nuclear war they fade into the background.* In the foreground stands Pope John Paul II, a sturdy and reliable ally.[14]

The very notion that philosophical, social, and theological differences simply "fade into the background" before war is, no doubt, merely a contemporary form of nihilism and materialism. That the Holy Father stands for quite a different position is something we shall attend to later on (Sections X and XI). But what is interesting here is the application of a consistent political strategy based on argumentation to ally the religious tradition of the West to marxist causes under the overarching blessing of presumably avoiding nuclear war or establishing "peace."

The real issue, therefore, is not really "war," but this particular strategy which uses war to promote military and political objectives. In a review of two British books on nuclear war in *The Economist*, there was a passage which, perhaps inadvertently, put this whole issue in context: "The fundamental weakness of the unilateralist case is to assume that there is nothing to choose between the international behaviour of western democracy and Soviet totalitarianism".[15] Thus, we do not have to be oblivious to Western problems and faults to recognize the far greater kind of dangers that arise under a more alien system. *The Times* of London also put the matter in the correct context:

> Obviously total disarmament would end all wars but that is utopian. Unilateral disarmament can save a particular country from the ravages of conflict but not from subjugation, death and destruction. The best way to avoid war is to avoid either miscalculation or giving others cause to miscalculate. This requires alert politics and the preservation of military balance.[16]

How to find a practical way to prevent war while preserving freedom and democracy is a twofold task. Yielding the latter to achieve the former is precisely the path of nihilism, particularly if, as Hannah Arendt suggested, it can be achieved without firing a shot.

The Economist's pointed analysis remains basic in this context:

> It is not plausible to argue that NATO's attempt to restore the nuclear balance in Europe increases the risk of nuclear war. It is the West's emerging inferiority in nuclear weapons which creates the possibility of a Russian attack. . . . That attack would pretty certainly include the use of nuclear weapons, if the Russians thought such weapons would clinch the issue. . . .
>
> The argument of the unilateralists . . . is upside down. They contend that the choice lies between a near-certainty of nuclear war if you have nuclear weapons, and a mere possibility of living under the Russian shadow if you do not. The truth is the reverse.
>
> The pro-nuclear lobby has to be honest and admit that, so long as nuclear weapons exist, the risk of their being used cannot be wholly eliminated. But that risk will not vanish until all these instruments of horror disappear from the face of the earth. Until that great day comes, if it ever does, the best way of reducing the risk of nuclear weapons against you is prevented from doing so by the knowledge that you can strike back in kind. That means keeping the nuclear balance. For western Europe, the real choice is then between a very small risk of war, if you keep the balance, and a near-certainty of entering the shadow of Russian power if you do not.[17]

The correct order of intelligibility, then, is not to begin with an analysis of weapons as physical things and then finally to interpret the issue of freedom as a secondary and subordinate question, but rather to understand that the freedom question with its consequent relation to politics *is* the one that determines the existence and the nature of the weapons.

One further point should be stressed in this approach. This concerns the question of whether the "striking back" is somehow only to be conceived as a sort of inevitable destruction of the planet and therefore immoral, or whether it is to be conceived as a measured, accurate military strategy directed at an enemy's offensive system.[18] Edward Luttwak's statement of the issue is very pertinent, since he, with considerably more realism than we are accustomed to read, pointed out that a successful banning of nuclear weapons would in all likelihood mean a renewal of so-called "conventional" war, only this time with all the added "improvements" of the past forty years. Since wars are not caused by "weapons," as Margaret Thatcher correctly reminded us, aggression will most likely follow if the deterrence is removed.[19] Furthermore, weapons are becoming more accurate. It has been a long time since the policy has been "massive destruction" rather than selective destruction of an enemy's military potential.[20] Luttwak wrote:

> Deterrence does not rest on the theoretical ultimate of allout population destruction. Whether nuclear or not, the workings of deterrence depend on the threats of punishment that others will find

believable. This requires that the act of retaliation be in itself pur-
poseful, and less catastrophic rather than more. And indeed ... the
nuclear arsenals have become steadily *less* destructive than they used
to be, as weapons have become more accurate. The total mega-
tonnage of our strategic nuclear forces is nowadays perhaps one-tenth
of what it was twenty years ago.[21]

There are two points to be made here—the first that nuclear
weapons will not be used if they are used as a clear political-military
deterrent, the second that the weapons in question do not have to be
conceived as primarily and only planet-destructive to achieve their
primary political deterrent function.

Luttwak then brought up the perplexing question, almost never
faced squarely in the "peace" and anti-war literature: namely, that
nuclear deterrence has worked, while its unilateral abandonment on
the basis of religious or moral scruple would itself *not* guarantee
either its non-use or the non-use of conventional warfare, and would
abandon others who depend on deterrence to the ravages of un-
deterred conventional war. This latter consequence, itself in the
very logic of the argument, brings out a most disturbing result, one
implied by Strauss, Cropsey, and others: namely, the dubious
willingness to sacrifice a whole civilization in the name of a mis-
conceived moral ethic incapable of conceiving anything higher than
survival at any cost.[22]

Rather than *risk* in any smallest way their own lives and those of
their children in a nuclear conflict, however improbable, they (the
anti-nuclear proponents) are in fact prepared to see others and their
children die in large numbers and by a certain outcome (in conventional, non-prevented war).
Those who thus frankly admit that they would abandon all the
nations that now rely on our nuclear enhancement for their security,
even if much death and war would inevitably result, are the most
honest members of the antinuclear camp. They have no moral pre-
tensions and no shame to drive them into hypocrisy and false argument. But what are all those rabbis and priests, pastors and bishops,
doing with them, standing in their crowds and singing their songs? By
what doctrine of theology, by what theory of morality, by what rule of
ethics is it decreed that the small risk of nuclear war is a greater evil
than the virtual certainty of the large-scale death in great-power wars
no longer deterred?[23]

The conclusion that can be drawn from this argument, then,
seems to be that clear-sighted nuclear deterrence, placed in the context of political persuasion, does practically work precisely to
"deter" both nuclear and conventional war, whereas its abandonment guarantees neither "peace" nor the non-use of conventional or
nuclear weapons. As a military or political policy, deterrence does
not address itself directly to a moral, religious, or rational discus-

sion of how the antagonisms of men and ideologies can be resolved or lessened, however much this is or is not possible. But deterrence or coercion *does* make such latter discussion at least possible at another level, as Plato had already sensed in Greek theory. The nihilism, materialism, and sense of necessitarian history that prevents man from understanding and living his values—the basic difference between democracy and totalitarianism—ought not to be permitted to "win" either by *war*, nuclear or conventional, or by *argument*, which would use "peace" to justify all or parts of mankind embracing the worst regime. The deterrence argument, on the other hand, is based on a solid, perceptive understanding of human nature. Its realism grasps that not even the worst ideologues will embrace the nothingness of death implicit in their own theories.

The Causes of "Peace" Movements

To discuss precisely the intellectual origins of the so-called "peace" movement of our time—to contextualize it, so to speak, so that we can make some sense about just why this widely heralded controversy should happen to arise at *this* particular time—we should distinguish two rather different sorts of issues. The first is, what actually prevents nuclear weapons from being used in concrete circumstances, in the given political conditions of our era? The second is, whose political interests are served by the particular manner in which the current discussion about war is being presented? Is it possible that the debate in the West about nuclear weapons (a debate that does not take place in the Soviet Union) is itself rather an instance, at least in many cases, of someone else's foreign policy being skillfully designed to obviate the very successes of deterrence policy? On April 30, 1982, in the UN Economic and Social Council, the East German, Cuban, and Hungarian representatives introduced practically identical resolutions seeking to identify the "right to life" movements with current Soviet policy which is seeking to prevent, as it was put, "any misuse of scientific and technological achievements for the imperialist arms drive, against the development of ever new inhuman weapons of mass destruction and against the growing neo-colonialist plundering of the developing countries".[24] Obviously this is an effort to enlist the "right of life" movements in the service of current goals of Soviet foreign policy, which seeks to prevent any adequate response to its own arms build-up.

This can be confirmed in another way by noting the response the Soviet broadcaster Vladimir Ostrogorskiy gave to Cardinal Josef Hoeffner's position that there is no one or clear way presently to guarantee binding peace, whether by unilateral advanced concessions or by mutual and balanced disarmament. Seeking to enlist Christian peace movements in the cause of immediate Soviet interest, Ostrogorskiy said, in a broadcast to Germany on August 30, 1982:

> This is why I get confused whenever appeals are made to secure peace through disarmament that exclude the issue of stationing new American missiles in the Federal Republic. On the one hand, any sincere call for common sense, peace, and disarmament is naturally welcome. On the other hand, one must also not overlook the danger that although fair words may ease the conscience of the supporters of peace and disarmament and give them the satisfaction of having done something for their cause, the arms race continues as planned by those who hope to derive financial and political benefit from it. In my view, there is only one way to guard against this danger: namely, to concentrate efforts in all countries on preventing projects such as the missile decision from materializing.

Clearly, this is an overt attempt to enlist the Western churches and peace movements in the ranks of current foreign policy objectives.

No one has stated the issue better than Prime Minister Margaret Thatcher, at the recent Disarmament Conference at the United Nations:

> Nuclear weapons must be seen as deterrents. They contribute to what Winston Churchill called "a balance of terror." There would be no victor in a nuclear exchange. Indeed, to start a war among nuclear powers is not a rational option. These weapons succeed insofar as they prevent war. And for 37 years nuclear weapons have kept the peace between East and West.
> That is a priceless achievement. Provided there is the will and good sense, deterrence can be maintained at substantially reduced levels of nuclear weapons. Of course, we must look for a better system of preventing war than nuclear deterrence. But to suggest that between East and West there is such a system within reach at the present time would be a perilous pretence.[25]

Mrs. Thatcher's remarks take on added weight since they come from an actual politician, one directly responsible for all possible consequences should this deterrence fail. The most likely result of such a failure would not be the destruction of the peoples of the earth by nuclear explosion, but their subjugation to a worldwide absolutist system.

Too often, the current discussion about nuclear war, when it does not arise out of sources directly traceable to Soviet foreign policy, comes from a sort of abstract analysis of weapons as "things," as if somehow "things" were themselves evil, rather than from an analysis of weapons as *political* instruments within a judgmental context of nature of the enemy, his ideology, of strategy, of human nature. Mrs. Thatcher went on:

> The fundamental risk to peace is not the existence of weapons of particular types. It is the disposition on the part of some states to impose change on others by resorting to force. . . . Let us face reality. The springs of war lie in the readiness to resort to force against other nations, and not in "arms races," whether real or imaginary. Aggressors do not start wars because an adversary has built up his own strength. They start wars because they believe they can gain more by going to war than by remaining at peace.
>
> The causes which have produced war in the past have not disappeared today, as we know to our cost. The lesson is that disarmament and good intentions on their own do not insure peace. . . . The security of our country and its friends can be insured only by deterrence and by adequate strength—adequate when compared with that of a potential aggressor.[26]

The British Prime Minister here spoke within the careful tradition of Augustine and Cicero and Aquinas, one which requires the political leaders responsible for peace and war to know exactly what they are up against. This is a view which prevents a kind of naive utopianism from being passed off as what accounts for human motivations in ideological times. Too, this enables politicians to avoid the implicitly Manichean view that things are "evil" in themselves, while allowing them to retain their capacity to address the question of how to confront those who would use force unjustly. Force, in itself, is not wrong or evil in politics.

Religious Materialism

If we would avoid the danger of identifying "evil" with material things rather than locating it in the wills energizing political controversy, we need again to reflect on Mrs. Thatcher's perception: "However alarmed we are by those weapons, we cannot disinvent them. The world cannot cancel the knowledge of how to make them." Likewise, we should resist the temptation of confusing rhetoric involving the theological problem of the "end of the world" with discussions about contemporary warfare, as if the two questions were the same sort of thing. No one has been more to the point on this topic than C.S. Lewis. The identification of the physical destruction of the world with a given level of moral evil present in it is a very questionable one. Lewis would today be surprised to find religious leaders especially, on the question of nuclear war, very close to the notion that the end of the human race is the "ultimate evil." The End of the World is not a merely physical thing. The world shall end naturally by the normal working out of the laws of the cosmos. This is not an evil. We know of the cycles of suns and planets. Lewis, however, pointed out that the world will end by God's decree, of which we know nothing in itself. "I can imagine no man will look with more horror on the End than the conscientious revolutionary," Lewis wrote in his remarkable essay, "The World's Last Night," "who has, in a sense sincerely, been justifying cruelties and injustices inflicted on millions of his contemporaries by the benefits he hopes to confer on future generations: generations who, as one terrible moment now reveals to him, were never going to exist".[27] The effort to identify a humanly established political moment or action with the eschatological end confuses realms and suggests that we can understand God's ways in this sphere.

"The doctrine that war is always a greater evil seems to imply a materialist ethic, a belief that death and pain are the greatest evils," C.S. Lewis wrote penetratingly in another context.

> Nor am I greatly moved by the fact that many of the individuals we strike down in war are innocent. That seems, in a way, to make war not worse but better. All men die, and most men miserably. That two soldiers on opposite sides, each believing his own country to be in the right, each at the moment when his selfishness is most in abeyance and his will to sacrifice in the ascendant, should kill each other in plain battle seems to me by no means one of the most terrible things in this very terrible world. Of course, one of them (at least) must be mistaken. And of course war is a very great evil. But that is not the question. The question is whether war is the greatest evil in the world, so that any state of affairs which might result from the submission is certainly preferable. And I do not see any really cogent arguments for that view.[28]

This remarkable passage of C.S. Lewis, as far as I can judge, has put the subject in its proper context. It has raised the question of the degree to which certain popular anti-nuclear or anti-war arguments are themselves rooted in philosophic materialism. Much of the contemporary literature on war, often including that coming from religious sources, has failed to remember the teaching of the Christian faith about human life in its transcendent sense. Instead of indicating some higher destiny for each person, whenever he might end or how, we have the kind of materialism Lewis indicated, the kind that is rooted in the Hobbesian notion that death is the worst of evils so that any political order based upon its avoidance is to be accepted. It seems strange, but as far as I know, in all the discussion about the possibility of complete nuclear discussion, no religious leader has undertaken to say much of anything to guide his spiritual flock in facing the possibility of death during a nuclear war. The lack of such discourse probably means that not even committed anti-nuclear, world-destruction Cassandras believe that nuclear war will come about.

Thus, if Margaret Thatcher reminds us about things and the use of things, C.S. Lewis reminds us of the danger of a materialism that can pass under the lofty rhetoric of preventing war, of the danger of confusing the unknown End of God's plan for the human race—the hour of which we know not (Mt. 24:42; 1 Thess., 5:2)—with an apocalyptic interpretation of the imagined use of weapons. We are beings meant for eternal life, and this world is to end—whether consumed by some passing planetoid, some cooling of the sun, or by some mistake of nuclear fission, or by some act of man, perhaps even one man. The question is not whether our end is the worst of all evils, but what is our destiny *however* we end. And this, in part, is revealed by how we live: whether we suggest by our living that nothing else is worth anything but the continuation of living on this earth, no matter under what circumstances. About our destiny, ironically, we seem to hear less and less in proportion as we hear that the ultimate "evil" is some potential "self-destruction," which is very unlikely to happen. The theories that place our happiness and emphasis on some perfect world down the trial of time are themselves the ones that obscure the moral questions that actually do occur in the lives of most people, ones which decide their personal destinies.

The Polish Poet Laureate, Czeslaw Milosz, put the matter in some proper perspective:

> The illusion of a country in which intellectuals dictate is very old and goes back to Plato. The intellectuals want to impose their philosophy. They want to eat, to make money, to make love, and to get on with life. But thinkers would transform these people into angels dedicated to pure intellect. This is behind the desire to transform the world, and it is a very dangerous illusion. Intellectuals in Marxist states do not rule; they are instruments of petty and vicious politicians.[29]

This hint that we search for our own form of salvation, demanding another kind of man than the one created and given, the one that in fact as we know him wants "to get on with life," is likewise behind the inability to understand the real nature of something like the Soviet regime, the actual one that is described to us by those who have actually lived under it.

In many ways, one major intellectual origin of recent "peace" movements is their tendency to think out of existence the actual Soviet regime and its methods. The nuclear threat comes from that regime, because of its ideological theories about aggression and history. The actual political causes are replaced by an abstraction relating to the thing-ness of weapons, so that the actual motives and powers cannot be confronted and thereby deterred. Vladimir Bukovsky is very perceptive here:

One of the most serious mistakes of the Western peace movement and of its ideologists is the obdurate refusal to understand the nature of the Soviet regime, and the concomitant effort to lift the question of peace out of the context of the broader problem of East-West relations. After several decades of listening to what they believe to be "anti-Communist propaganda," they have simply got "fed-up with it." They ascribe everything they hear about the East to a "cold-war-type brainwashing," and make no attempt to distinguish what is true from what is not. This attitude, which I can only ascribe as a combination of ignorance and arrogance, makes them an easy target for any pseudo-theory (or outright Soviet propaganda) that happens to be fashionable at any given moment. . .

The Communist rulers unscrupulously exploit the tragedy of the Soviet people in World War II for the purpose of justifying both their oppressive regime and their monstrous military spending. They try their best to instill into the people a pathological fear of the "capitalist world." Fortunately, the people are sane enough to laugh at the very idea. Thus, contrary to this theory, there is no paranoid population demanding to be protected in the Soviet Union, despite the best efforts of a perfectly sober and cruel government.

No, it is not the fear of invasion or a World War II hangover that has driven the Soviet rulers to wage an underclared war against the whole world for half a century now. It is their commitment—repeated quite openly every five years at each Party Congress since the beginning of this century—to support the "forces of progress and socialism," to support "liberation movements," everywhere on the globe.[30]

Both Bukovksy and Dorothy Rabinowitz, moreover, have quite carefully noted the striking pattern that occurs when suddenly "peace" movements appear in western Europe and the United States and particular objectives of Soviet policy.[31] What this means, in other words, is that the task of preventing war and in some radical sense of improving the fate of the Soviet and other peoples under this regime is not likely to be found in some "higher" philosophic system or some mystical "peace" movement, but in the concrete work of politics, of the Augustinian sort of politics which can account for threats, weapons, strategy, and coercion. It should be one that avoids what Milosz called the "dangerous illusion" of seeking for some utopian place, while neglecting the real conditions of human life and what actually exists within its confines. To maintain that it is "awful" that we should have to account for coercive politics in this fashion comes very close to the proposition that Creation is badly made.

The Defense of Deterrence

The Central Committee of the German Catholics, at the Conference at Bad Godesberg (November 17, 1981), caught much of the kind of thinking that ought to be operative here. The German document repeated Margaret Thatcher's point that arms do not cause war while accepting Bukovsky's notion that ideology must be taken into account. The clash in Europe for the past thirty-five years

> was not caused by the fact that the adversaries have been, or are armed, but by a clash of opposing political views and interests. It is this clash and the mutual distrust which are responsible for the ever higher levels of armaments of the powers involved.
>
> However open we Christians need to be for new developments leading towards a greater measure of freedom and self—determination, and however much we pin our hopes on them, for the present the following continues to hold good: the conflict between the communist and the democratic states is essentially due to the fact that the communist side subordinates its policy, both internally and externally, to the command of the totalitarian ideology of Marxism-Leninism. It is an ideology which, in fundamental questions, disregards the ethical norms and misuses the basic concepts that have developed in European philosophical and theological thinking, and, over the last two hundred years, have given the liberal, democratic and constitutional state its shape. Marxism-Leninism knows no spiritual and social pluralism and no tolerance. It is symptomatic of this attitude that in the Soviet sphere of power an open discussion of security policy is not tolerated.[32]

The German discussion likewise emphasized the meaning and importance of precisely *politics*—"any ethical demand made on politics must acknowledge the *specific laws inherent in politics* and take them into account in considering and reaching a decision."[33]

This, moreover, is why weapons cannot be treated merely as "things" with imaginary results, however graphically described, which, on analysis, decide "morality." It is rather the pressures of valid "politics" which will enable the control of arms and force to be guided in a safer direction, not abstract analyses of what "might" come about.

> It is vital to remind oneself that weapons have not only a military but always a political function as well. In the case of nuclear weapons, it is obviously the latter function which plays a decisive role. We can see how the danger inherent in these weapons triggers fears that have an impact on political thinking. Nuclear weapons can be used to bring pressure to bear particularly on those states which do not have them, making them politically tractable.
>
> If it does not want to find itself in such a situation, the only course open to the Western alliance, by way of a response, is to equip itself with comparable weapons within a collective security system. Only in that way can it defend itself against political coercion and make it clear to a potential aggressor that the attempt to translate his intentions into reality by the use of force entails considerable risks for him as well. That is essentially what the policy of deterrence is all about. It aims at making it clear to an adversary that the trouble and

expense of launching an attack or an attempt at coercion are out of proportion to the benefit to be derived from such an action and are therefore not advisable. The French term for this concept is "dissuasion." More effectively than the German word, "Abschreckung," or the English equivalent, "deterrence," it places the issue at stake into the proper political context. Under the given circumstances, then, nuclear weapons too are a means of preventing war and thus of maintaining peace. Without a *quid pro quo* and without a reasonable chance of making peace secure in other ways, it is impossible to dispense with them.[34]

This sort of realism is the context out of which reduction of arms might come about in any meaningful sense. Both the German document and the Papacy talk in this fashion. This is why also, from a strategic marxist viewpoint, the "peace" movement, which heightens the "scare" about weapons in the abstract, is mostly designed as a way to prevent the kind of deterrence and therefore limited peace that have effectively worked to confine the marxist system, at least militarily.[35] This puts a new light on the question.

Another basic element in this discussion has to do with the understanding of freedom, with what life in a totalitarian system is like. As the German scholars, writing in *Foreign Affairs*, put it, bluntly: "The protection of a free society based on the rule of law is just as important a part of a policy of preserving peace as the preventing of war. War can always be avoided at the price of submission."[36] Everyone is, of course, aware that many recent statements, also from ecclesiastical sources, are prepared to accept this latter proposition, the "ethics" of submission, on a variety of dubious grounds. Some say the marxist system is the best anyhow, or that it is the "wave" of the future. Others claim that no weapons of any effective deterrence capacity can be used, so better suffer evil than to do it. Still others maintain that western freedom is a sham and give some sort of ideological explanation which accounts for everything except why people always escape *out* of marxist systems, never *into* them. Again, the German Catholic Document is to the point:

> The alternatives being offered to a peace policy based on a balance of forces are unconvincing. They play down the frightening consistency of totalitarian thinking. . . . In the final analysis, therefore, these alternatives promote a kind of thinking ultimately leading to the destruction of political peace in freedom. People who think in that way fail to realize that political peace in freedom does not merely provide us with an environment in which it is very pleasant to live, but that political peace in freedom is the very prerequisite for a life of human dignity. Where this realization is gradually disappearing and where people cannot visualize the extent to which life under a

totalitarian system is devoid of human dignity, a breeding ground develops for those active minorities who merely use the word peace and the longing for peace as a vehicle for asserting their own totalitarian or anarchistic goals that are opposed to freedom. Where the fatal tendency to disregard history is combined with political ignorance, an insufficiently developed ability to make ethical distinctions, as well as the reluctance to fight actively for our common peace order, such minorities can gain an influence that far transcends their real importance.[37]

In Western philosophic tradition, the idea of surrender to the worst regime has never been thought to be an act of virtue, nor has the inability to distinguish the worst regime been considered an act of high intelligence. As C.S. Lewis remarked, it seems more like rank materialism wherein a religion or an ethic has forgotten what discourse about human life is like.[38]

Immorality and Surrender

Perhaps the best statement of what is really at issue, why we deal here with an argument about the intellectual soul of civilization itself and of religion's relation to this argument, was stated by Professor Joseph Cropsey in his brilliant essay, "The Moral Basis of International Action":

> Perhaps it will be said that there can be no victory where there are no survivors. This is true enough, but inconclusive. The question is, What follows from it? The most obvious conclusion is that we must do our utmost to insure that plenty of us will survive, so that the nation can go on in the enjoyment of victory. But it might be argued that no one could possibly survive the next war, which must come to an end with the apocalyptic death of the human race. Let us for the present accept this assumption as empirically correct. Then there must not be a next war. To argue so is plausible, but again inconclusive, for the argument tells us nothing about the form in which the cost of avoiding war must be paid. It might be that we pay for peace by abject surrender. That is unthinkable. It is unthinkable because the argument in favor of doing so is based upon the premise that, morally and politically, nothing matters—nothing, that is, except survival. The proper name for this position is not philanthropic morality but nihilism without intestines. The fortified species of nihilism also argues that nothing matters—except success. We have lost contact with the human spirit if we can no longer sense the repulsiveness of nihilism and the depravity of it in its emasculated form. If nothing matters, then human life does not matter. (Who would mourn it?) If anything matters, it is the decency of life and the possible self-respect of men. Still, where there is life, there is hope for some amendment of any evil. We agree, and recommend the thought to our enemy; it deserves his consideration no less than ours. In brief, there is one cost of avoiding war which is more than we can afford: subhuman abasement.[39]

Professor Cropsey has here, of course, again brought out the sort of nihilism and materialism that C.S. Lewis also noted in the thinking about war. And like Lewis, Cropsey understands the relation of this question to that of the End of man taken as a species.

Thus, the proposition that we should continue on this Earth for as long as possible, no matter under what political conditions—this taken as a first principle of morality for deciding questions of war and peace—this is indeed materialism and nihilism in the purest of forms. Cropsey continued:

> It is a paradoxical and fearful fact that the only way we might have peace is by opening our minds to war. That way lies the presumption of safety—in war, if it comes, through peace if it does not. It is not necessary to say that there is no guarantee that mankind will not be decimated and irradiated. Nature itself does not vouchsafe his survival to man: the instruments of general destruction of which we now stand in dread are inferences from principles implicit in nature, principles which have lain in darkness from eternity, waiting to be grasped and put in execution by man. We happen to be the climactic generation, in whose time the combination of man and nature seems to be achieving the critical mass. We cannot avoid our fate, but we need not be craven in confronting it. On the contrary, the ways of danger and moral decay are one. Life itself hangs by the thread of honor.
>
> We seem to have concluded that the dictate of morality coincides with the interest of men and nations whose purposes are compatible with freedom and high-mindedness. This conclusion was the one intended.[40]

Here, with some relief, perhaps, we find the realism of a Margaret Thatcher, the active, sensible politician, combined with the perception of a C.S. Lewis, in a political philosophy directed against a kind of materialism and nihilism that masks as virture before the problem of war in our time. We can, indeed, call this materialism a kind of "high-minded immorality," which by a certain specious rigor of argument becomes a tool for justifying the worst regime in the name of religion and ethics. Our era, in other words, has a great need for an ethic that does not lead society into tyranny.

Papal Thought on Deterrence

We are, then, by now sufficiently aware that certain religious people, including evidently several Catholic bishops, have substantially embraced the thesis that unilateral disarmament is "morally" necessary. Paradoxically, here we usually mean American disarmament. We can, no doubt, certainly be *for* unilateral disarmament—that of the Soviets first—but there does not seem to be any such movement in the Soviet Union itself. Other bishops, not willing to go quite so far, have inaugurated a series of "anti-war" parish seminars, in which the horror of such a possible war are presented, usually with little balanced effort to present the case for deterrence. Scholars in the future, it seems, would do well to begin collecting the content and ideological directions of these seminars being pushed in the local parishes in various parts of the country. Needless to say, the looseness and often one-sidedness of these presentations have caused great concern among the laity as well as among reponsible politicians, who recognize the dangers to national security should a large segment of the population suddenly "opt" for an anti-war doctrine. The Soviets too recognize this significance.[41] The early drafts of the proposed American episcopal statement seem reluctantly to grant some deterrence capability without seeming to have any adequate political or moral foundation for it. Thus, it does not take a political genius to figure out who profits if one side suddenly throws down the one type of arms that counts or professes a doubt about whether any defense is possible.

At this point, then, it seems worthwhile to pay some attention to the considerably more cautious manner in which John Paul II has approached this issue. This seems strikingly unattended to, even in—or better, *especially* in—the religious press. Though he is a man of peace, expected to deplore the dangers of war, recognizing that means of civil defense are not his area of competence, the Pope is also a Pole, who saw what losing a war meant both in terms of destruction and imposed ideology. At the same time, it is quite unfair and simply unscientific to think that democratically elected public officials in the free world, responsible by public mandate for the legitimate defense of their own and other people, do not share his concern, word for word, as he has spelled it out at the United Nations, Hiroshima, and countless other places.

John Paul II never speaks of unilateral nuclear disarmament as a moral imperative. Nor does he suggest that a simple analysis of the bomb as a thing itself is sufficient to decide the question. Like every political leader, including the Soviet rulers, the Pope knows the very existence of such weapons is dangerous and, therefore, "ought" to be adequately controlled. But he understands very clearly also that this cannot be a one-sided affair or an excuse to impose, by pretending moral scruple, an absolute rule on a people in the very process of pretending virtue. Here, it is well to cite the Holy Father's most recent comments, on the assumption that the earlier ones are already readily available.[42] On December 13, 1981, after he had sent a delegation of scientists and medical men to several leaders of states to give them a description of the most probable effects of a nulcear war—knowledge, as the Holy Father

understood, they certainly already appreciated as well as he did—
the Pope went on:

> I have, in fact, the deep conviction that, in the light of a nuclear
> war's effects, which can be scientifically forseen as certain, the only
> choice that is morally and humanly valid is represented by the reduc-
> tion of nuclear armaments, while waiting for their future elimination,
> carried out *simultaneously* by *all commitment* of accepting *effective*
> controls.[43]

Clearly, these are not the words of a unilateral disarmer or a naive
cleric who does not know his enemy. Presumably, if any one of the
conditions cited by the Holy Father could not be verified—simultaneous, all parties, explicit agreements, effective controls—then
no responsible political leader ought to proceed to remove his
effective deterrence.

Freedom and Deterrence

John Paul II's most elaborate and careful treatments of this
problem were in his Message for the World Day of Peace, January 1,
1982, and his Message to the U.N. Disarmament Conference, June
11, 1982, the latter Message delivered by Cardinal Casaroli, the
Papal Secretary of State. In the first Address, the Holy Father
noted that the greatest cause of contemporary unrest is not
weaponry as such, but it arises from the "application of certain concepts and ideologies that claim to offer the only foundation of the
truth about man, society and history."[44] It takes little imagination to
suspect what he might have had in mind. But the Holy Father sent
out a very serious caution to those joining the "peace" movement
with very little appreciation for the nature of weaponry, ideology,
or politics. "Scientific studies on war, its nature, causes, means,
objectives and risks have much to teach us on the conditions of
peace."[45] The Pope evidently thought that such studies can contribute to demonstrate the need for negotiations, but his words also
warned of the immense dangers of "politicizing" the religious side of
the war question by intimating that this is merely a simple question
of a few local meetings and petitions to national leaders, in those
countries where such activity is still allowed.

"Although Christians put all their best energies into preventing
war or stopping it," John Paul II reflected, "they do not deceive
themselves about their ability to cause peace to triumph, nor about
the effect of their efforts to this end."[46] John Paul II is optimistic
enough to suspect that we are not "determined" to have war. He is
not a believer in marxist historical necessity. He has read Augustine
too. He has understood that we must account for our personal

destiny even if we fail to prevent war. He has indicated eloquently to us that life on Earth ends for all of us soon enough, and this is our destiny, even our hope. He still teaches a Christian catechesis. Thus the Pope does not confuse, as many religious people seem to do, the "worst" evil with physical death, whether all at once or one at a time.

In a marvellously clear challenge to any simple view of the situation, John Paul II spoke of the Christian mind addressing itself to this subject, but in terms valid, it would seem, for any reasonable person:

> Christians are aware that plans based on aggression, domination, and manipulation of others lurk in human hearts, and sometimes even secretly nourish human intentions, in spite of certain declarations of a pacifist nature. For Christians know that in this world a totally and permanently peaceful human society is unfortunately a utopia, and that ideologies that hold up that prospect as easily attainable are based on hopes that cannot be realized, whatever the reason behind them. . . . Christians are convinced, that these deceptive hopes lead straight to the false peace of totalitarian regimes.[47]

Here, the Holy Father noted the problem of "false peace," which we earlier saw in Aquinas. And, to be sure, if we read these extraordinary lines of common sense carefully, we are only too well aware that many, without the "personal experience" of a Pope Wojtyla, do *not* realize what this false "peace" of a "totalitarian regime" might be like.[48]

John Paul II then recalled that even while trying to prevent every kind of warfare, still, in the name of an elementary requirement of justice, "peoples have a right and even a duty to protect their existence and freedom by proportionate means against an unjust agressor." The theory of the just war, in other words, is by no means obsolete. But do "proportionate" means include a nuclear or bacteriological attack? The Pope was very careful. What he does *not* say is that the right to defend oneself is wrong. He affirms, on the contrary, that it is a "right" to defend oneself, "which is only real in principle," but that these weapons ought to lead to an "effective means of negotiations." War is no way to resolve our conflicts if we can help it and we can. And this merely reiterates the Pope's position on mutual, assured disarmament. If negotiations with valid terms and with mutual agreement and controls do not reasonably come about, the alternative is *not* nuclear pacifism, but the continued and measured balance of weapons in a political context, which insures their non-usage. Under the cover of disarmament, people are *not* to be subjected to an alien power, particularly a totalitarian one. The Pope is clear on this point. These approaches, then, indicate the very objective, responsible attitude of the Holy Father with regard to nuclear weapons in their political reality, the one best designed to assure their non-use.

Deterrence and Negotiations

In the June 11, 1982 U.N. Disarmament Message, the Holy Father retained his direct, rational, realistic approach. There were no dramatic appeals to "better red than dead," no calls for unilateral pacifism. There were no one-sided analyses of the dangers which exist nor was there any lack of understanding about military, political, or spiritual matters. Again, the Pope does not hold that wars are caused by "arms."

> The production and the possession of armaments are a *consequence* of an ethical crisis that is disrupting society in all its political, social and economic dimensions. Peace, as I have already said several times, is the *result* of respect for ethical principles. *True* disarmament, that which will *actually* guarantee peace among peoples, will come about only with the resolution of this ethical crisis. To the extent that the efforts at arms reduction and then of total disarmament are not matched by parallel ethical renewal, they are *doomed* in advance to failure.[49]

Here, the Holy Father again reminds us of the tradition that peace is a *result*, that the causes of wars lie deeper than arms themselves, that behind any lasting peace must come a viable discussion of concepts of right and duty.

In defining his own position, then, John Paul II rejects any "determinism," self-interest, naivete, or ideology as the proper context in which we can talk of peace or disarmament. Weapons and conflicts are products of a "spiritual confusion born from narrow-minded self-interest or by defence of ideological claims" (#12). The fact that such things exist means that responsible politicians must account for them in their own terms. In the very act of suggesting the dangers from ideology or naivete or self-interest or theories of determinism, Pope Wojtyla reminds us that such things exist as facts of our world which will not immediately go away. It is in this context of realism that he has sought to carve out his own position, one that begins with the positive affirmation, against any theories of despair, determinism, or pure pragmatism, that "Peace is not a utopia nor an inaccessible ideal nor an unrealizable dream. War is not an inevitable calamity. Peace is possible."[50] These are not just pious words. Many clerics, including bishops, have seemingly been telling us that "war is inevitable." And what characterizes John

Paul II's alternative is its careful attention to all the elements—political, military, social, philosophical, and spiritual—that go into making "peace possible." We need to hear such words against the "peace at any cost" school of thought, perhaps more than against the cynical pragmatist who is skeptical about the whole project.

First of all, in describing his alternative, John Paul II in his U.N. Message on Disarmament stated the strict practical military preparedness position in both its classical—"*Si vis pacem, para bellum*" —and in its contemporary form: "the balance of terror," to which Margaret Thatcher referred. The Pope does not reject the temporary necessity of this latter thesis when historical judgment of actual politicians deem it prudent, but he does warn of its long-term instability when deeper conflicts are not confronted (#3). He first noted that we must hold that peace is possible, a reaffirmation of the doctrine of human freedom, so that any thesis of a "balance of terror" is not rooted in a theory of man which would imply that human nature is corrupt or predetermined. The alternate approach must be stated in this fashion, then: "Total disarmament, which is mutual and surrounded by such guarantees of effective controls that gives to everyone confidence and necessary security". The Pope's optimism is very guarded. The practical alternative that the Holy Father has in mind, then, uses words like "guarantees" and "effective controls" and "security," the very stuff of political prudence.

The Holy Father clearly understands that this issue is "a complex one where a number of values—some of the highest order—come into play". He also reminds us that this is, for the most part, a practical area, practical in the Aristotelian sense, "where there are divergent viewpoints that can be expressed." The complexity of this area can be oversimplified at great peril to any true peace. The Holy Father, recounted the Church's teaching in this area since the beginning of the atomic age. This teaching has sought to remind men of "the disastrous effects of war" and the need to find measures and appropriate structures "to ensure the legitimate security of every people". The Pope understands that the other side of a lack of legitimate security is a loss of freedom. He summarized the Church's basic position carefully, a summary that ought to appear in every religious discussion of the topic:

> The teaching of the Catholic Church in this area has been clear and consistent. It has deplored the arms race, called nonetheless for mutual progressive and verifiable reduction of armaments as well as greater safeguards against possible misuse of these weapons. It has done so while urging that the independence, freedom and legitimate security of each and every nation be respected.[51]

Thus, there are political, military, ethical, and spiritual elements, each of which has a proper and necessary place.

John Paul II, likewise, has recognized the dangers when "peace" movements are used for other purposes.

> However, it is one thing to recognize the interdependence of questions; it is another to exploit them in order to gain advantage in another. Armaments, nuclear weapons and disarmament are too important in themselves and for the world ever to be made part of a strategy which would exploit their intrinsic importance in favour of politics or other interests.[52]

Such a passage speaks volumes in its nuanced way of warning about the use of "peace" movements for ideological purposes.[53] The Pope would hope to give the benefit of doubt to the legitimacy of recent movements, but he remarks:

> The ideological bases of these movements are multiple. Their projects, proposals and policies vary greatly and can often lend themselves to political exploitation. However, all these differences of form and shape manifest a profound and sincere desire for peace.[54]

Discussions of "peace," then, are not exempt from the burden of what those actually participating in them stand for and how they are used.

John Paul II, then, directly faced the question of deterrence, in a basic passage, wherein he showed his capacity to locate and distinguish military, political, and practical elements.

> In current conditions "deterrence" based on balance, certainly not as an end in itself but as a step on the way toward a progressive disarmament, may still be judged morally acceptable. Nonetheless, in order to ensure peace, it is indispensable not to be satisfied with this minimum which is always susceptible to the real danger of explosion.[55]

The Pope, then, understands what politicians like Margaret Thatcher face and argue. He calls the military side of this position a "minimal" solution, meaning that it is a starting element—required by the ideological problems that lie behind weapons, but to be used as a basis for negotiations, based on the realism which the weapons' reality forces on practical politicians of whatever ideology. The Pope also understands that "conventional" weapons are today still the greater and more likely source of problems.[56] Thus, retaining deterrence and a consciousness of the importance of freedom and security, within the context of a realistic end aimed at practical disarmament, the rational means of "negotiations" are possible, but not very easy and not to be engaged in naively.

Today once again before you all I reaffirm my confidence in the power of *true* negotiations to arrive at just and equitable solutions. Such negotiations demand patience and diligence and must notably lead to a reduction of armaments that is balanced, simultaneous and internationally controlled.[57]

Again, these are questions of fact, of verifiability, of pressure, of realism. When the conditions are *not* present in the judgment of wise and experienced men responsible for the public order, they do not have to pretend they are.

Conclusion

To conclude, then, we can suggest that whatever we hear from the religious sector, for all its perplexity, about the morality or immorality of war or nuclear deterrence, we need to be reminded that there is a strong voice in our political culture as well as in the Church, including that of the Holy Father, that knows and comprehends the nature of both nuclear weapons *and* totalitarian systems, that seeks to contain *both*. The means proposed to do this include politics, economics, diplomacy, armies, philosophy, and religion. Particularly, we do not want to place ourselves in an intellectual position whereby we permit ourselves to fall under the totalitarian systems *because* of some kind of supposedly "moral" thinking about weapons, taken in political isolation, which would dictate surrender and force the worst regimes on all peoples. This latter eventuality would be an enshrining of nihilism and materialism within mankind under the name of virtue, the danger of which perhaps was the very first question treated by Western political philosophy.

The outlines of what is possible for us, realistically confronting the factual basis of increasing Soviet power and the real nature of its system, make it necessary to think *politically* about weapons, so that they will not be used *either* to impose a totalitarian system on yet another people, without a shot—the Pope is a Pole and understands this danger—*or* to be dropped by anyone, especially because countervailing weakness made the temptation to do so irresistible, something Margaret Thatcher eloquently warned about. Alexander Solzhenitsyn already warned in 1975 of the danger of allowing Soviet nuclear superiority to reach a stage of four or five to one and the ensuing demand to give up. Many seem intellectually prepared to give up on what they consider moral or religious grounds. There is, however, considerable question about whether the recent "peace" movements have always arisen for purely intellectual or moral reasons and not as an instrument in a policy seeking political objectives. This would suggest that the danger is not so much the abstract one of weapons but the concrete one of freedom, as writers like Vladimir Bukovsky have suggested. Thus, the far safer and more realistic way to prevent war, in the present context, is to keep our "dissuasion" dry while always being ready to look into more fundamental issues of ethic and religion. The minimum remains, a strong military component, while working for effective, verifiable, reasonable controls.

G.K. Chesterton wrote an essay in the beginning of this century called "About Beggars and Soldiers," in which he addressed himself to those theories that held we ought to eliminate beggars by establishing a perfect economic system and soldiers by a perfect political system. Such very noble ideas, as Samuel Johnson reminded us, are very dangerous for us "finite human beings." We need to be much more careful, much more concerned about what we can do ploddingly, strictly, in the meantime. Chesterton, as usual, caught just the right touch:

> Nobody wants anybody to beg or anybody to fight. But when promise after promise of universal peace is broken, and conference after conference abandons the task of establishing international justice, is it so very odd that some people should still want something to defend national justice, in the sense of justice to their own nation? And if the beggar and the soldier seem to remain, *since* they seem to remain— then I do most strongly feel that it is better that they should not be regarded merely as blots or pests, but rather in the light of the traditional virtues associated with the tragedy; the one in the light of charity and the other of chivalry.[58]

This remains mostly our condition and certainly our situation. It seems far saner to accept it and work on its basis than to presume that "universal peace" and "international justice" are already established among us.

Ambassador Jeane Kirkpatrick, at a recent lecture in Washington, remarked that the reason the peace-keeping instruments of the United Nations do not work is because there are powers who do not want them to work.[59] Behind the institutions and instruments of national and international policy lies the question of philosophy, ethics, and the understanding of what human nature and personhood are about. John Paul II has shown a very clear perception of the relation of these deeper problems to the inability of mankind to reduce arms and promote a more peaceful world. He maintains peace is not a utopia, but his descriptions of how it is to be achieved acknowledge the careful accountability and balance that the so-called political realists demand. In so far as the intellectual origins of the "peace" movement are ideological or insincere, we do well to avoid them. On the other hand, a view of man and his capacities that is merely deterministic or founded on the view that he is fully evil cannot be the proper climate of negotiations or progress. While we can admit that much is wrong with human performance that must be honestly faced, we need to teach that this is not a full view of man's dignity. On the other hand, if our emphasis on human value seems rooted merely in survival or materialism, it will ultimately appeal to no one. The current climate in which the nuclear debate has arisen has, it would seem, some very suspect origins. On the other hand, if it is used to clarify what is at issue, as people like Margaret Thatcher, Professor Cropsey, the German Catholic Committee, John Paul II, and many others have done, then the cause of *"vera pax,"* of true peace, will be greatly advanced.

FOOTNOTES

1. Midge Decter, "Barbara Tuchman's Alternative to History," *Contentions*, June 1982, pp. 1-4.

2. Herbert Deane, *The Political and Social Ideas of St. Augustine.* New York, Columbia University Press, 1963. See also John East, "The Political Relevance of St. Augustine," *Modern Age*, Spring 1972, pp. 167-181.

3. Karl Rahner, "Peace," *Theological Dictionary.* New York, Herder, 1965; p. 342.

4. Harry Jaffa, "The Politics of Freedom," *Statesmanship.* Durham, N.C., Carolina Academic Press, 1981, pp. 1-9. See also Charles N.R. McCoy, *The Structure of Political Thought.* New York, McGraw-Hill, 1963.

5. James V. Schall, "The Reality of Society According to St. Thomas," *Divus Thomas*, no. 1 (1980), pp. 13-23.

6. Aleksandr Solzhenitsyn, Addresses of June 30, 1975, and July 9, 1975, to AFL-CIO; Washington, D.C., American Federation of Labor, 1975. Also *Solzhenitsyn at Harvard*, edited by Ronald Berman; Washington, D.C., Ethics and Public Policy Center, 1980. *Cf.* Igor Shafarevich, *The Socialist Phenomenon*, New York, Harper and Row, 1980, and Vladimir Bukocsky, *The Peace Movement and the Soviet Union*, New York, Orwell Press, 1982.

7. Leo Strauss, *On Tyranny*, Chicago, University of Chicago Press, 1963, p. 225.

8. *Ibid*, p. 226.

9. *ABN Correspondence*, (Munich), July-October 1982. Also Bukovsky, *The Peace Movement*, and Dorothy Rabinowitz, "The Building Blocks of the Freeze Movement," *Wall Street Journal*, June 10, 1982.

10. Hannah Arendt, *On Revolution*, New York, Viking Press, 1965, p. 7.

11. Solzhenitsyn, Addresses.

12. Jean-Francois Deniau, "La Detente Froide," *L'Express*, Paris, September 10, 1982, p. 91.

13. Thomas Molnar, "Socialism, Si; Kung, No," *National Review*, August 20, 1982, pp. 1022-1024. Also Dale Vree, *On Synthesizing Marxism and Christianity*, New York, Wiley, 1976.

14. Carl Marzani, "The Vatican as a Left Ally?" *Monthly Review*, July-August 1982, p. 40. Italics added.

15. *Economist*, London, "Nuclear Sense and Nonsense," July 12, 1982.

16. *The Times*, London, "Man and His Weapons," editorial, June 24, 1982.

17. *Economist*, London, "They Are Wrong," October 17, 1981, pp. 11-13.

18. Karl Kaiser *et al.*, "Nuclear Weapons and the Preservation of Peace," *Foreign Affairs*, Summer 1982, pp. 1157 ff.

19. Margaret Thatcher, Address to the UN Disarmament Conference, *New York Times*, June 24, 1982.

20. Kaiser, "Nuclear Weapons," and Seymour Weiss, "The Current Debate Over Nuclear Arms," *Wall Street Journal*, April 20, 1982.

21. Edward N. Luttwak, "How to Think About Nuclear Weapons," *Commentary*, August 1982, p. 28.

22. Joseph Cropsey, "The Moral Basis of International Action," *Political Philosophy and the Issues of Politics*, University of Chicago Press, 1977, pp. 172-188.

23. Luttwak, "How to Think."

24. Economic and Social Council of United Nations, Statements of German Democratic Republic, Hungary, and Cuba, on the Right to Life on Report of the Human Rights Commission, April 30, 1982.

25. Thatcher, Address.

26. *Ibid.*

27. C.S. Lewis, "The World's Last Night," *The World's Last Night and Other Essays*, New York, Harcourt Brace, 1960, p. 111.

28. C.S. Lewis, "Why I Am Not a Pacifist," *The Weight of Glory*, New York, Macmillan, 1980, p. 43.

29. Czeslaw Milosz, "Interview with Nobel Laureate," *Natinal Catholic Register*, June 13, 1982.

30. Bukovsky, *The Peace Movement*, pp. 41, 47.

31. *Ibid.*, pp. 20-22, and Rabinowitz, "The Building Blocks."

32. Central Committee of the German Catholics, "On the Current Peace Discussion," Conference at Bad Godesburg, November 17, 1981. English translation by Frau Hofheinz, Deutscher Bundestag, WO1- 0507 - 31. German text in *Frankfurter Allgemeine Zeitung*, November 17, 1981, p. 6.

33. *Ibid.*

34. *Ibid.*

35. Bukovsky, *The Peace Movement;* Rabinowitz, "The Building Blocks"; Kaiser, "Nuclear Weapons."

36. Kaiser, "Nuclear Weapons," p. 1165.

37. Central Committee, "On the Current Peace Discussion."

38. C.S. Lewis, "Why I Am Not"

39. Cropsey, "The Moral Basis," pp. 184-185.

40. *Ibid.*

41. Bukovsky, *The Peace Movement;* Rabinowitz, "The Building Blocks."

42. *Peace and Disarmament*, Documents of the World Council and the

Roman Catholic Church. Rome: Pontifical Commission on Justice and Peace, 1982.

43. *op. cit.*, p. 43. italics added.

44. Pope John Paul II, "World Day of Peace Address," *L'Osservatore Romano*, English edition, January 4, 1982.

45. *Ibid.*

46. *Ibid.*

47. *Ibid.*

48. Shafarevich, *The Socialist Phenomenon.* Also Solzhentizyn, Addresses.

49. Pope John Paul II, "Negotiation: Only Realistic Solution," Message to Special Session of United Nations for Disarmament. *L'Osservatore Romano*, English edition, June 21, 1982.

50. *Ibid.*

51. *Ibid.*

52. *Ibid.*

53. Joseph A. Harriss, "Karl Marx or Christ (on World Council and Peace)?" *Reader's Digest*, August 1982, pp. 130-134. See also Arnaud de Borchgrave, "World Peace Council," *The Economist*, London, July 3, 1982, p. 4.

54. Pope John Paul II, "Negotiation."

55. *Ibid.*

56. Cf. Luttwak, "How to Think."

57. Pope John Paul II, "Negotiation."

58. G.K. Chesterton, "About Beggars and Soldiers," *Selected Essays*, London, Metheun, 1949, p. 72.

59. Jeane Kirkpatrick, Address on the United Nations. Delivered at the Capitol Hill Club, Washington, D.C., September 17, 1982.

The Amorality of Arms Control

Thomas F. Payne

Ever since nuclear weapons were introduced into the world in 1945, their massively destructive power has posed a dilemma for both moral theorists and strategists. On the one hand, nuclear weapons seem to violate the principle of proportionality: the doctrine that the means employed in pursuit of a given end must be proportionate to the ends sought. This principle is not only a moral one, but a strategic one as well, and it is a problem for the strategist, no less than for the moralist, to outline circumstances in which it is clear that the evil to be avoided by warfare is greater than the evil of the destruction that war would wreak. On the other hand, once nations have nuclear weapons, it also seems that the only defense available against them is to threaten retaliation in kind against any nation that would make use of them. This leads to a growing perception among moralists that the only solution to the nuclear question lies in arms control. The purpose of this paper is to examine the demand for arms control as moral and political advice. Before that demand can be fully accepted, a number of questions must be answered. How good a thing is arms control, from the point of view of both strategy and of justice? What prospect do arms control negotiations hold forth for achieving nuclear disarmament, and for reducing the risk of catastrophic war? What is a good-faith effort at arms control; and is good faith all that is needed for successful arms control negotiations? If something more is needed, what is it?

Before addressing these questions directly, it will be necessary to say something about the just war theory. Earlier in this century, the German sociologist Max Weber drew a distinction between the ethics of intention and the ethics of responsibility. Augustine's teaching about the just war is to be placed in the second of these two categories. Augustine teaches that war may be made for the sake of preserving political communities, because political communities are among the goods God has created in this world. Augustine's teaching also recognizes that man's life on earth entails choosing between greater and lesser evils more often than it does choosing between absolute good and absolute evil. The just man, the responsible man, is the man whose choices, on balance, bring about more good than evil in the actual affairs of men and states. Therefore, Augustine can justify war as a means of preserving the political community, because he can envisage circumstances in which the destructiveness of war—an admitted evil—is a lesser evil than the destruction of civil society, the loss of justice within the society, or the loss of a society's freedom.

This must be kept in mind when one considers arms control as a means of escaping the dilemma of nuclear weapons. Arms control efforts cannot be judged solely in terms of the peaceful intentions of those who promote them. If arms control is morally superior to armaments, arms control must protect the political goods that men seek to protect by arming. That is to say, arms control efforts, in order to be a morally superior alternative to nuclear deterrence, must be able to produce peace, the security of states, and the freedom of peoples. And they must be able to do so in the world in which we now live. Otherwise, they have no value, as either a practical or a moral alternative.

Arms Control in Theory

Whenever arms control is discussed, either as a body of doctrines or as a series of practical measures, it is a good idea to distinguish it from disarmament, a concept with which it is frequently linked. (By disarmament, in this case, I mean total disarmament—not nuclear disarmament, which is a type of arms control measure.) The disarmament movement has a goal which is quite distinct from that of arms control. Arms controllers have always seen their purposes in strategic and technical terms, but "disarmament" is entirely a political affair. There is quite obviously no way in which nations, or mankind generally, can be disarmed, because weapons are whatever comes to hand when there is fighting to be done. Disarmament, or the abolition of war as a means of resolving conflict, requires either the eradication of the desire to fight or the erection of a world government to frustrate that desire. In short, disarmament is a utopian aspiration.

Arms control theorists and practitioners, as they see themselves, stand as models of realism and practicality alongside disarmers. They do not appeal to the idealism of nations, but to their self-interest. In particular, they appeal to the supposedly common interest of all nations to avoid the destructiveness of modern warfare, both nuclear and nonnuclear. Their object is not the uto-pian abolition of war but the creation of "a stable strategic environ-ment" in which 1) the costs of preparing for war will be less onerous, 2) the outbreak of war through accident or miscalculation less likely, and 3) the destructiveness of war less catastrophic, should war break out. Strategic stability itself is a concept with two compon-ents: crisis stability and arms race stability. Crisis stability between rival nations or blocs of nations is said to be achieved when they are so armed that in a political crisis, neither side can gain an advantage over the other by striking first. In such a strategic envi-ronment, neither side would be tempted to resolve a political crisis by a sudden initiation of hostilities (since neither side can gain a decision by a first strike). Moreover, since each side knows that the other does not have an effective first strike, no side will attempt a preemptive strike of its own. Under conditions of crisis stability, so the argument goes, nations will not be prevented from going to war, but if they do, the decision to take that drastic step will be as deli-berate as possible, and not the product of despair over a deteriora-ting military situation, miscalculation of a rival's intentions and capabilities, or accident.

Arms race stability, the second component of strategic stability, is achieved when rival nations are no longer improving their forces in order either to achieve a destabilizing first-strike potential or to foil the achievement of a first-strike capacity by other nations. De-stabilizing improvements in armed forces might be the simple aug-mentation of armaments, or the technological modernization of armaments. Arms controllers consider the latter more dangerous than the expansion of armed forces, because changes in technology can put the existing armed forces of nations in jeopardy of a first strike much more quickly than the mere augmentation of forces. For this reason, arms-control theories tend to be biased against tech-nologically advanced powers.

In pursuit of strategic stability, arms controllers have produced a large body of highly technical doctrine which has attempted to define the kinds, numbers, and deployments of weapons which are to be regarded as "destabilizing." However, if the arms control project is to be successful, negotiators must be able to elicit agree-ments between nations in the absence of an international political climate conducive to strategic stability. This qualification may seem merely obvious, but it is important nonetheless. Arms are seldom the cause of disorder within the international community. They are the symptoms of disorder. If the political atmosphere is tranquil, if the outbreak of a destructive war is not forseen or forseeable, why negotiate arms control agreements? They would be little more than memoranda detailing the existing force structures of the nations involved. To be of value, arms control agreements must be able to create strategic stability, reduce the chance of war, and increase the security of nations during times of prolonged international political tensions and instability.

Unfortunately, the ability of arms control agreements to produce these results in the circumstances of prolonged international instability is extremely limited. The track record of the arms control project is not a good one. However, before examining any particular example, it would be prudent to state in general the reasons for the frequent disappointment of arms control expectations, lest the impression be created that circumstances peculiar to particular cases have lead to the unsatisfactory results. The poor track record of arms control in this century has not been caused by any want of skills or diligence on the part of arms control negotiators or on the part of theorists guiding their policies. Rather, the arms control project itself is an essentially flawed undertaking; its chief defect is to advance the notion of an apolitical (or amoral, if you will) strategic stability, defined in technical terms. Of course, this statement needs to be expanded upon and defended.

Causes of Instability

If it is conceded that armaments, arms racing, and even war itself are not the causes of disorder in the international political system, but merely the symptom of disorder, a question necessarily arises as to the nature of the disease which produces these symptoms. To answer, one might begin by turning the question around and asking when the international system is inclined to peace. History and logic suggest that two conditions must be present. First, the international system must be regarded as legitimate—that is, there must be agreement among the powerful states as to what are the acceptable goals of foreign policy and the acceptable means of pursuing them. Second, the legitimate order must be enforced by a balance of powers such that any state or combination of states which transgress beyond the boundaries of the legitimate order will be resisted by an equally powerful state or combination of states. In an international system enjoying these attributes, rivalries between states tend to be limited to competition for marginal advantage within the established framework of order. The limited policies pursued by nations effectively limit the likely scope of their wars, and hence limit the extent of their armaments. Most international disputes are susceptible to resolution through negotiation within the legitimate framework, because the issues contested are likely to be of marginal significance. Should negotiations fail and war come, it is likely to be of brief duration and limited violence, because no nation will exhaust either its treasure or its manhood in a prolonged war for merely marginal gains. For these reasons, in a stable international order, arms control agreements—although easy to conclude—are likely to be superfluous.

In marked contrast, periods of instability are characterized by the *loss* of an effective consensus for the regulation of international conduct. Nations become divided into *status quo* powers (those attached to the old consensus and the order it produced) and anti-*status quo* powers, either revisionist or revolutionary. The international moral consensus may be lost or become ineffective in two ways. First, a powerful nation may accept the prevailing legitimating consensus as just, but may come to regard the prevailing distribution of advantages as contrary to its own interests. In such a case, the anti-*status quo* power attempts to revise the international system in its own favor without destroying it altogether. Imperial Germany in the period before the First World War is a prime example of a revisionist power.

A second and more serious cause of the loss of legitimacy is the presence of a revolutionary power which rejects the legitimating principles of the international system as themselves unjust. The wars of religion of early modern times were the product of a revolutionary condition within the international system, because the claims to authority put forth by various Protestant princes could not be reconciled to the universal claims of Catholicism championed by the House of Hapsburg. In our own time, both Nazi Germany and Soviet Russia have challenged the "bourgeois" and "capitalist" nations of the West in the name of ideologies whereby they govern their own peoples.

In the presence of a revolutionary power, the system itself is at stake. Because the claims which revolutionary states make against other states are necessarily limitless, disputes are rarely solved through negotiations. The antagonists lack a common framework whereby rival claims may be limited and compromised. For this reason, international talks, whether formal or informal, tend to degenerate into posturings in which hostile governments try to demonstrate to third parties—and perhaps to their own citizens— the unreasonableness of their rivals' position. In such an atmosphere, international negotiations are generally a prelude either to war or to armament build-ups, and can rarely achieve more than an armed truce between exhausted antagonists.

Thus revolutionary periods in the international system are times of tension in which arms control agreements are far from superfluous—as they are in times of stability—but are almost impossible to achieve. The reasons are easy to understand. Anti-*status quo* powers acquire arms in order to achieve their destabilizing objectives either by force or by intimidation; *status quo* powers acquire arms in order to prevent anti-*status quo* powers from achieving their objectives. Since the anti-*status quo* power has made a deliberate decision to take up arms, it is not likely to relinquish them voluntarily, unless the *status quo* powers are willing to make concessions that violate their vital interests. Without a resolution of the underlying political conflict, limitations on armaments will not be in the interest of either *status quo* or anti-*status quo* powers; with such a resolution, arms limitations will be spontaneous.

Despite the unfavorable atmosphere for arms-control negotiations during unstable periods, such negotiations do take place. But the purpose which the antagonistic parties bring to the bargaining table is rarely that of finding a way to a secure, technically defined strategic stability, as arms control theory suggests it should be. During arms-control negotiations in periods of international instability and revolution, *status quo* powers tend to assign to their arms control policy the entire burden of improving relations with anti-*status quo* powers. For their part, anti-*status quo* powers attempt to use arms control agreements to shape arms competition to their own advantage. The presence of these incompatible objectives in arms control negotiations during revolutionary periods places the *status quo* power at a considerable disadvantage, especially if the *status quo* power is a liberal democracy. Arms-control negotiations provide the governments of anti-*status quo* powers with a platform to protest their peacefulness to the citizens of liberal democracies and to excite in them the hope of peace through arms-control agreements. The hopes of the citizens then become a powerful pressure on the leaders of liberal democracy to make strategically unwise agreements with their anti-*status quo* rivals. Thus it is no accident that during this century, the century during which the arms-control project has compiled its poor track record, the leading *status quo* powers have all been liberal democracies, and all have entered into unwise arms-control treaties.

Historical Precedents

What these reflections upon arms control predict, history confirms. The frustrated naval arms-control initiatives of the British before the First World War are good examples of the futility of attempting to deal with strategic problems, which stem from the political instability, by means of technical agreements on armaments. Imperial Germany was a revisionist power whose ambitions for a German-dominated Europe were blocked by the encircling Franco-Russian alliance. In order to break out of this encirclement, the Germans developed the famous Schlieffen plan, which called for a decisive first strike at the French through the Low Countries and the defeat of Russia in a subsequent and longer campaign. The delicate timing of the plan would be upset, however, if the British fleet intervened on the side of the Franco-Russian alliance. The German government was unable to obtain a promise of neutrality from the British against the event of a Continental war, and therefore, it decided to build the High Seas Fleet—a strategic weapons system designed to support the Schlieffen plan by making British naval intervention in France or the Low Countries either difficult or impossible.

The British responded with naval construction of their own—thus began the pre-war naval arms race—and diplomatic approaches to the Germans for a naval arms-control agreement. The German government was willing to enter into such an agreement only if the British promised neutrality in the event of a Continental war—that is, only if the British promised acquiescence in a change in the international status quo. For its part, the British government was unwilling to give up its freedom to intervene on behalf of the Continental *status quo* as its interests might require. No agreement was reached, therefore; indeed no agreement could have been reached without a change in the political interests of the two nations.

After the First World War, it became fashionable to believe that arms racing, rather than the intractable political problems which moved Europe to arm, was an important cause of the war. Therefore, the period betwen the wars was quite friendly to arms-control efforts, and a number of agreements were actually produced, among them the Anglo-German Naval Treaty of 1935. The Nazi regime which came to power in 1933 had rekindled and enlarged the ambitions entertained by the Kaiser. However, by the Treaty of Versailles, Germany had been stripped of the means of revising the international system, having been deprived of the right to maintain effective armed forces. When Germany began to rearm in violation of the Treaty, the British took no steps to oppose them, but rather approached them for arms-control negotiations, hoping that an arms-control agreement would reintegrate Germany once again into the international community on an equal (i.e. *armed*) footing without posing a threat to other nations. The result was the naval treaty, whereby Germany agreed to limit its surface fleet to one-third the size of the British fleet and to restrict its submarine fleet to 60 percent of British numbers until 1940—at which time Germany had the option of expanding its U-boat fleet to 100 percent of British strength. The Germans also promised never to use the U-boats against commerce, despite the fact that such a great number of submarines could have no other use in the face of overwhelming British surface superiority.

German participation here is a prime example of how a revisionist power used arms-control agreements to manipulate public opinion in a liberal democracy, so as to provide political cover for an arms build-up and to shape arms competition to its own advantage. The British, on the other hand, played the role of a *status quo* power placing unjustified hopes for improved relations upon arms-control negotiations. Having learned that Germany could not challenge Britain's superiority in surface ships, Hitler decided to compensate for British naval superiority by developing air power and submarines: two categories of weaponry in which Germans could compete successfully with the British. The British public—sensitized by history to naval threats, but having no memories of threats from the air—conceded air superiority to the Germans in the years following the treaty and failed to make the provisions for anti-submarine warfare which the German submarine fleet necessitated. For the British, the naval treaty signified the beginning of a political detente with the Germans. They continued the treaty as evidence of a mutual intention "never to go to war with one another again." Chamberlain cited it, together with the famous piece of paper signed at Berchtesgarten, on his return from Munich in 1938. Despite these good intentions, the treaty did nothing to address the political instability which German ambitions in Europe caused.

Deterrence in Europe

The explosion of atomic bombs over Hiroshima and Nagasaki in 1945 ended the Second World War and began the nuclear era. It was clear to all that this new weapon would profoundly influence military thinking and practice, but the precise implications of the new weapon system were unclear at that time, and to a large extent, they remain unclear. Opinions of all sorts were advanced and continue to be advanced. Of particular interest were the theories of a group of strategic thinkers, later to be called "the arms-control community," which saw the development of nuclear weapons as the occasion for renewed hopes for arms control. For them, the bomb was "the absolute weapon," a device of immense destructive power against which no military defense was feasible. In such an unprecedented military situation, it was easy to suggest that the only hope for the security of nations lay in the adoption of mutually deterring weapons systems.

However, if Hiroshima did mark the emergence of an unprecedented international strategic environment, the post-war political environment was altogether too familiar, as the unlimited claims of

Soviet Communism replaced those of Nazi Germany as a source of revolutionary instability. Moreover, despite the presence of the "absolute weapon," the application of arms-control efforts in the post-war world have shown the same pattern as that outlined above with respect to the Anglo-German naval rivalry. Several times during the post-war period, the United States, the world's leading *status quo* power, has gone to the arms-control bargaining table with a clear superiority in strategic nuclear weaponry and with the intention of halting the arms race. In time, as detente towards the Soviet Union became the official American policy, arms-control agreements became the chief evidence that hostility between the two superpowers was easing, and arms-control agreements came to bear the burden of improving Soviet-American relations.

The behavior of the Soviet Union with respect to arms control has also been according to predictable form. An anti-*status quo* power, indeed a revolutionary one, the U.S.S.R. has used arms-control negotiations to shape arms competition to its own advantage and to influence domestic opinion in the Western nations to the advantage of the Soviet Union. During the period of the Strategic Arms Limitation Talks, the Soviet Union has undertaken the greatest conventional and nuclear arms build-up in the history of the human race. It has tried, often successfully, to negotiate bans on categories of weapons in which the United States has an advantage or a vital interest. The two treaties which have emerged from the "SALT process" do little but ratify existing Soviet plans for arms expansion. But what is most wonderful of all, the Soviets have managed to engage in so ambitious a military program and so clever a use of negotiations, while maintaining the moral and political high ground. As a result, Europeans take to the streets to demonstrate against the Pershing IIs, despite the fact that it was German Chancellor Helmut Schmidt, not Jimmy Carter or Ronald Reagan, who first requested their deployment, and despite the fact that the American missiles (not yet deployed) have been proposed as a response to the Soviet deployment (already underway) of SS20's, one of the most destabilizing and threatening developments in the post-war arms competition.

In several key respects, of course, the Soviet Union and Nazi Germany, and their characteristic behavior, are different. The Soviet Union does not share the fascist infatuation with war as a uniquely worthwhile human endeavor, the preferred means of reaching international settlements. Nor do the Soviets make the same sort of immediately provocative territorial claims upon the *status quo* that Hitler did. For their part, the post-war *status quo* powers have been united in their opposition to Soviet ambitions, and (at least until recently) nothing like a party of appeasement has been influential among them. The key difference between the years before World War II and the post-war years, however, is this: the post-war Soviet Union does not seek to become the dominant regional power in Europe; it already *is* that power. Together with its allies, it has a commanding strategic position on the Continent, and it can defeat any other Continental power or combination of Continental powers. In order to prevent the Soviet drive for hegemony over Europe from reaching culmination, the United States has interjected itself into European affairs and, in effect, given a military guarantee to Western Europe. Its reasons for doing so are as much political as military. American military power compensates for European weakness, and American political leadership of the Western alliance serves to overcome the potentially divisive antagonisms of European nations for one another.

Although NATO is politically defensive in its purposes, throughout most of its history the NATO alliance has had neither the intention nor the capacity for pursuing a defensive strategy in the proper sense of the term. Despite its earliest plans, NATO has never built up a conventional force large enough to guarantee that any attack by Warsaw Pact forces across the line dividing Germany will fail. Instead, the Western alliance has adopted a strategy of deterrence, seeking to prevent an attack upon Western Europe by raising to an unacceptably high level the costs which the Soviet state and the Soviet military would have to bear in order to overrun the NATO forces stationed in the German Federal Republic.

In the early days of NATO, when the United States possessed a monopoly on nuclear weapons and later on the effective means of intercontinental delivery, deterrence was achieved by the threat of "massive retaliation" against the Soviets for any aggression. Later, as the Soviet Union developed an intercontinental strategic capacity of its own, and advances in weapons technology made smaller nuclear warheads possible, the doctrine of flexible—or graduated—response was developed. According to this newer doctrine, NATO would first respond to an attack upon its territories with conventional forces. Should these prove inadequate to halt a Soviet invasion, nuclear weapons stationed in Europe would be brought into action. These range from tactical nuclear weapons for use against front-line troops to intermediate-range ballistic missiles and bombers for use against basing, communication, logistic and other rear-echelon facilities. Finally, should the collapse of NATO resistance appear imminent, the intercontinental strategic arsenal of the United States would be used. This concatenation of weapons on the tactical, theater, and strategic levels is intended to deter Soviet military action, which might succeed at a lower level of violence by threatening to escalate the conflict to a higher level—one presumably unacceptable to the Soviets because of a clear American superiority at that higher level.

The policy of deterring war in Europe through the threatened use of nuclear weapons, like any policy, is open to criticism. Like any policy, it cannot be justified as a perfect choice, but merely as the best choice possible under the circumstances. Two circumstances in particular have influenced NATO's decision to deter a Warsaw Pact attack upon Western Europe rather than plan to defeat such an attack in a conventional battle. First, the Western democracies have been unwilling to maintain conventional forces large enough to fight a conventional, defensive battle for West Germany. Second, the West German government has been unwilling to countenance military planning which would make its territory the battleground required by a defensive strategy.

Strategists have questioned the wisdom of deterrence on purely military grounds, with much of their criticism centering upon two related questions: "What if deterrence fails?" and "What if deterrence itself is deterred?" It is entirely conceivable that what American planners see as damage unacceptable to the Soviet Union may be acceptable to them if it were the price of dominating Western Europe. It is also conceivable that the Soviets might possess superior nuclear forces at any of the levels of nuclear combat envisaged by the doctrine of flexible response. In such a case, American nuclear deterrence would lose its credibility, because the launching of American weapons at that level would bring greater destruction down upon NATO forces, including American forces stationed in the continental United States, than the supposedly deterrent weapons of the United States would inflict upon the Soviets. Should either of these two unhappy contingencies materialize, deterrence would have failed, and NATO commanders would find themselves in the unenviable position of having to fight a war with forces designed for an entirely different purpose—forces inadequate not only for deterring, but also for fighting a war.

American deterrent policy also has an inherent political vulnerability. The problem is common for every military alliance, and concerns the sharing of the military burdens and the distribution of the military risk. Quite understandably, Western Europeans (especially the West Germans) would like to see American deterrent forces so configured that the burden of deterring Soviet aggression would be borne by the intercontinental strategic forces of the United States. As Henry Kissinger has put it, they would prefer to see a nuclear war fought with missiles flying over their heads, even if the purpose of the war were the defense of Western Europe. Conversely, and again quite understandably, American strategic planners would like to configure the West's deterrent forces in such a way that a resort to the intercontinental forces in the United States would be delayed as long as possible. In order to do this, they seek to augment the deterrent value of weapons stationed in Europe. European governments, for their part, tend to resist American plans for beefing up the West's arsenal of deployed tactical nuclear weapons on the grounds that it tends to make nuclear combat in Europe more likely and more destructive. In sum, the Western alliance tends to divide on the question of who is to be the primary target of Soviet nuclear fire: the United States or Western Europe.

Any discussion of Soviet military policy toward NATO must begin by making clear how different Soviet strategic thinking is from our own. The concept of "deterrence," which is the virtual cornerstone of Western strategy, is unknown to the Soviet military lexicon. Its absence is hardly a matter to be wondered at. Deterrence is a policy attractive only to satisfied, *status quo* powers seeking to prevent changes. Therefore, deterrence is a strategic policy attractive to NATO. The Soviet Union, on the other hand, seeks to change the *status quo* and has developed its strategic doctrine accordingly. All Soviet forces, conventional and nuclear, are organized and equipped so as to enable the Soviet Union to fight and win a war for the control of Europe. Should war come again to Europe, Soviet operational doctrine calls for the Soviet forces stationed in Eastern Europe and the western Soviet Union to assume the initiative as soon as possible, assuming, of course (unrealistically), that they had not already taken the initiative by beginning the war. Soviet armored and mechanized infantry units, equipped to operate on a nuclear battlefield and supported by massed artillery, would penetrate the NATO front at selected points and begin a drive towards the Rhine. As front-line units became exhausted, rear-echelon units would be brought up in order to maintain the momentum of the attack. The pattern of the Soviet offensive would resemble a number of spear points thrust through the protective barrier of the NATO front lines and into the West German heartland, the spearpoint being continually renewed with fresh units brought up from the rear. In a relatively short time— some estimate as little as 72 hours—the Soviet spearheads would reach the Rhine, and the struggle for political hegemony over Western Europe would be over.

Soviet military doctrine also calls for the use of nuclear weapons at all levels of combat, in a number of mutually complementary roles. First, they would be employed to augment the firepower of conventional Soviet artillery along those segments of the NATO front selected by Soviet commanders for penetration. Second, Soviet medium—and intermediate—range weapons would strike deep into NATO territory, destroying communications and logistic facilities, air bases, ports, arsenals, and other rear-echelon installations. The purpose of these strikes would be to stun and paralyze NATO forces, thus enabling the Warsaw Pact forces to achieve the surprise which Soviet military doctrine holds indispensable for successful offensives on the nuclear battlefield, while at the same time impeding the ability of NATO forces to organize resistance to Soviet thrusts.

Finally, in the background of this scenario of war would stand the intercontinental strategic missiles of the Soviet Union. Their primary mission would be to prevent their counterparts in the United States from fulfilling their deterrent function. In other words, they aim to deter the deterrent. However, it would be a mistake to assume on this basis that the deterrent mission of Soviet strategic forces means that they are the mirror-image of American strategic forces. American forces are designed to deter attack by threatening a retaliation which would make a successful attack excessively costly. Soviet doctrine, on the other hand, calls for the deterrence through war-making capacity. In other words, Soviet doctrine requires that Soviet missiles have the capacity to attack and destroy American strategic forces before they can be launched, so that Soviet conventional and theater nuclear forces in Europe can have a free hand with NATO forces without having to worry about a retaliatory nuclear attack from the continental United States. In sum, then, whereas American nuclear policy has sought to cancel the political advantage that conventional strategic dominance in Europe has given the Soviets, Soviet strategic policy tries to cancel the cancellation—or deter the deterrent, or more accurately, destroy the deterrent—in order to take advantage of their superiority. It is for this reason that the Soviets have built up the offensive power of their missile forces far beyond anything required by American theories of deterrence.

However, if Soviet military doctrine requires that Soviet forces have an assured war-making capability and the capacity to take offensive action, this fact does not support the hasty conclusion that the Soviets plan an attack upon Western Europe, either in the forseeable future or after a continued build-up of their forces. Of course, scholars, journalists, and other commentators have constructed a number of scenarios in which the Soviet leadership launches an attack on Western Europe out of desperation, as the Soviet strategic position in Europe begins to deteriorate or as domestic crises threaten the Communist regime in Russia itself. These scenarios are not entirely implausible, but their very premises lead to the conclusion that the Soviet Union would attack Western Europe only out of desperation, and as a last resort.

Rather than being the intended instrument of a direct attack upon Western Europe, the war-making capacity of Soviet armed forces serves the Soviet anti-NATO strategy of intimidation. In time, so the Soviet leadership calculates, the awesome mass and firepower of the Red Army will demonstrate to the governments of Western Europe that it is dangerous to be friendly to the United States and hostile to the Soviet Union. When such a conviction becomes current—or perhaps it would be more accurate to say, "as it becomes current,"—Western Europe would become progressively more receptive to Soviet political, economic, and security initiatives designed to diminish American influence in Europe and ultimately to exclude American armed forces from the area. In short, the war-making capacity of the Soviet Union is primarily intended to serve as the basis for an offer the Western Europeans cannot refuse.

Arms Control in Practice

In retrospect, more than a decade of Soviet-American Strategic Arms Limitation Talks makes it abundantly clear that the Soviet Union's participation in arms-control negotiations has been governed by the spirit of arms competition, not arms control. The Soviets have not sought to cooperate with the United States in order to create a "stable strategic environment" as Western arms control theorists have defined that term. Rather they have attempted—and successfully—to manipulate the Western desire for such an environment, in order to gain political and military advantage. Their specific objectives have been: first, to undermine the NATO alliance by playing upon divergences between the security interests of the United States and its European allies; second, to provide political camouflage for their massive armament programs while forestalling possible Western counter-measures; and third, to cancel Western advantages in arms technology by securing arms control agreements which would limit American rights to develop and to deploy technologically advanced weaponry.

Conversely, American behavior at SALT has conformed to the pattern normally exhibited by *status quo* powers. It has gone to the bargaining table not only in search of "strategic stability," but also in search of improved political relations with its superpower rival. At times—for instance, at the time of the signing of the SALT I Treaty—American policy-makers have behaved as if they believed that arms competition was the cause, rather than the symptom, of deteriorated political relations between the United States and the Soviet Union. Thus successive American governments have signed arms control agreements which cannot be justified on the basis of strategic criteria, but only on the assumption that improved relations with the Soviets would ensue. As the anticipated improvements in Soviet-American relations have failed to materialize, the United States has found itself in a deteriorated strategic posture in the face of the massive Soviet military build-up.

What ultimately came to be known as "the SALT process" began in 1965, some number of years before "SALT" became a household word, when Secretary of Defense Robert McNamara decided to halt the American deployment of ICBMs at 1054 in order to create the preconditions for a controlled and stabilized strategic environment. At the time, the Soviets had approximately one-third that number of ICBMs, all of inferior quality in terms of accuracy, but were expanding their force rapidly. McNamara saw this not as a threat, but as an opportunity to escape the dilemma of the nuclear age through a renewed application of arms-control theory, specifically the doctrine of mutually assured destruction. He believed that strategic stability would be achieved when each nation achieved a force sizeable enough to survive an attack upon itself and to retaliate against the attacker, inflicting unacceptable damage. The United States already had such a capacity with its ICBMs, submarine-launched ballistic missiles, and B-52 manned bombers, and according to the official view, if the Soviets were to acquire a similar capacity, the deployment of offensive arms could be frozen by an arms-control agreement guaranteeing strategic stability and security for both sides.

After the Soviets were persuaded to join the SALT negotiations by the Johnson Administration, their invasion of Czechoslovakia postponed the start of the talks until the beginning of the Nixon Administration. These talks, known to history as SALT I, were not originally conceived as the first step in a series of negotiations over differing aspects of strategic arms. They were intended to issue in a comprehensive treaty imposing limits on all types of strategic arms. The first difficulty which the talks faced, however, was a dispute between American and Soviet negotiators as to what the term "strategic" comprehended. The Soviet position was that an offensive strategic weapon was any delivery vehicle capable of carrying a nuclear weapon to the home territory of either nation. Thus they considered FB 111 fighter-bombers stationed in Europe as offensive strategic weapons, whereas American military doctrine called them theatre weapons for use in the defense of Europe. To the Soviets, these weapons were "forward based systems." If the Soviet definition of the scope of the talks had been accepted, American theatre nuclear weapons would have counted against any treaty-imposed limit on offensive nuclear weapons, while Soviet theatre nuclear forces would *not* have counted against the numbers permitted to the Soviet Union. This would have left the Soviets a free hand in the deployment of nuclear weapons against the European nations of NATO, whereas the United States would have been faced with a series of painful decisions as to whether or not to invest in its intercontinental nuclear strike forces at the expense of theatre nuclear forces. Very likely, over the long run American policy makers would have preferred the defense of the continental United States to the forward deployment of weapons into Europe; therefore, the ultimate result of American acceptance of the Soviet definition of strategic weaponry would have been the subversion of the Atlantic community.

Once the scope of the talks was settled, two influences shaped their outcome, the ABM (anti-ballistic missile defense system) debate in the United States and the Nixon Administration's decision to pursue detente with the Soviet Union aggressively. From the beginning of the talks, attempts to set an upward limit on Soviet offensive weapons, to match the unilateral restraint of the United States, went nowhere. The interest of the Soviet negotiators attached itself almost exclusively to the defensive missile systems under consideration for deployment by the United States. Considerable controversy had been generated concerning the potentially destabilizing role ABM systems might play in a strategic environment formed—or about to be formed—by the doctrine of mutually assured destruction. On the one hand, it was argued that ballistic missile defense systems promoted strategic instability. A nation with an effective system might be tempted to strike first in a crisis, relying upon its ABMs to ward off the "stabilizing" effects of its adversary's retaliatory second strike. On the other hand, ABM proponents claimed that ballistic missile defense systems would contribute to strategic stability by protecting retaliatory forces from a disarming first strike. The ensuing debate was decided not so much on the strategic merits of the issue (indeed, one wonders how arms-control and deterrence theories could supply the criteria necessary to settle it) as by the politics of the time. In the mood created by the Vietnam War, the public was ill disposed toward proposals for new weapons, preferring instead to trust in negotiations and diplomacy for its security. Moreover, given the Soviet position at the arms limitation talks, it was widely believed that building a ballistic missile defense system was inconsistent with the possibility of improved relations with the Soviet Union.

Therefore, it became clear that any treaty emerging from SALT would severely limit the deployment of ABM missiles, but it remained unclear whether the treaty would be comprehensive in the American sense of the term, *i.e.* whether it would include limitations on offensive weapons. This issue was becoming more and more urgent as time passed, because SALT had not slowed the Soviet deployment of ICBMs. During the period of the talks, they approached, then surpassed, the number of ICBMs deployed by the United States, exceeding the number required for a secure second strike and disappointing the expectations of many in the arms-control community. If the United States were to give up ballistic missile defense for the sake of strategic stability, then some limitation on Soviet offensive power seemed necessary in order to preserve American retaliatory forces from a destabilizing vulnerability; but the Soviets continued to reject any concrete proposals advanced for that purpose.

Again, political influences external to the negotiations—in this case the imperatives of detente—became decisive. Fresh from their famous trip to the Great Wall of China, Nixon and Kissinger engaged the Soviet leadership directly in negotiations in Moscow, without reference to the official negotiators in Helsinki. The result was the separation of the issue of defensive arms from that of offensive arms. A treaty of unlimited duration, the SALT I ABM Treaty, was signed, severely curtailing the rights of both nations to deploy ABMs. It was accompanied by a pact of limited duration and less binding authority: the SALT I interim agreement on offensive arms. This instrument, good until 1977 (when it was expected that a formal treaty on offensive arms would have been concluded) limited the number of ICBMs on each side to those already deployed, while the Soviets were permitted to complete their plans for upgrading their fleet of ballistic-missile submarines. In addition, the modernization of ICBMs by increasing their offensive effectiveness with multiple warheads of greater accuracy was permitted.

The SALT Experiments

When the SALT I Treaty was presented to the Senate for ratification, its accompanying interim agreement attracted more discussion than the treaty itself. The agreement's concession to the Soviets of superior numbers in offensive strategic launchers was justified on two grounds. First, treaty proponents argued that while the Soviets were permitted more missiles (and by indirection, a heavier aggregate throw-weight), their superiority in offensive power was not as great as casual inspection of these measures might lead a naive observer to suppose. By and large, it was said, Soviet missiles were not as accurate as their American counterparts, and they were not equipped with MIRVs. Hence, they would be unable to knock out all the American ICBM forces on the ground. American forces were sufficient for deterrence: the surviving forces could strike back. Of course, this argument would be utterly invalidated if the Soviets should thoroughly modernize their missile forces, providing them with enough warheads of sufficient accuracy for a disarming first strike. Here the second justification of SALT I, a much more politically significant justification, came into play. So confident were they of the universally compelling reasonableness of the arms-control project that certain portions of the arms-control community argued that the Soviets' entrance into an arms limitation agreement meant that they had accepted American theories of deterrence, stability, and arms control in gross, if not in detail. In time, therefore, they could be expected to see the advantages of an agreement limiting offensive arms. Because of this expectation, the possibility that the Soviets would increase the offensive capacity of their ICBM force to threaten the American retaliatory capacity was not entertained seriously in some quarters, if it was not dismissed altogether.

The SALT II negotiations and their resultant treaty on offensive arms have utterly failed to fulfill the optimistic expectations engendered by the SALT I package. Although the treaty authorized the deployment of 2250 strategic nuclear launch vehicles (ICBMs, bombers, and submarine-launched ballistic missiles) and the MIRVing of no more than 820 missiles with no more than ten warheads apiece, these provisions can hardly be said to limit anything, least of all Soviet armament programs. There is a general consensus among students of defense policy that these figures are close to what the Soviets would have deployed in the *absence* of a treaty, and what is more important, that the Soviet arsenal includes enough warheads of sufficient accuracy and power to place the American Minuteman missiles in danger of a first strike. It was for this reason that in arguing for the ratification of the SALT II Treaty, the Carter Administration was in the odd position of having to promise to expand armaments by building a new survivable missile system. SALT II also permitted the Soviets to increase their arsenal of likely second-strike weapons by excluding the strategically capable Backfire bomber from the terms of the treaty. Some argue that the Backfire's exclusion was justified by the exclusion of the FB 111 fighter-bombers from the new treaty, but this is hardly convincing. As part of the strategic balance, FB 111 had predated the first SALT negotiations; the Backfires were newcomers, additional forces authorized by omission from the arms limitation treaty.

SALT II also imitated the pattern of its predecessor in attaching a subsidiary, provisional agreement to the main treaty, in this case the SALT II Protocol on cruise missiles. This agreement, together with certain provisions of the treaty, severely restricts the right of either power to test or deploy the technologically advanced cruise missiles of range greater than six hundred kilometers. Since the United States alone has the technical ability to develop such weapons, these limitations fall effectively only upon us. What is interesting about the restriction on cruise missile development (not merely deployment) is that there can be no objection to the deployment of ground-launched cruise missiles from the standpoint of the doctrine of mutually assured destruction. They are too slow to be used as first-strike weapons; hence the deployment of any number of them cannot threaten strategic stability. Indeed, the deployment of a large number of them should be an assurance of stability, because they would guarantee a second strike. The Soviets have sought to impede the development of such weapons and to restrict the development of an American ABM system for the same reason that they have sought an unfettered right to deploy offensive weapons of their own. They are not interested in assuring the United States of second strike, the canons of arms control and the doctrine of mutually assured destruction notwithstanding.

In retrospect, it now seems obvious that for the Soviets, the value of SALT has been the opportunity afforded to develop a first-strike capacity against the American homeland without having to overcome the massive obstacle of an America fully committed to arms competition. The elusive prospect of a controlled strategic environment, providing security without recourse to preparations for war, has disarmed public opinion in the West, blinding it to the implications of Soviet weapons programs.

The Senate's ratification of the SALT I ABM Treaty made the doctrine of mutually assured destruction official American policy. The United States would rely upon the deterrent effect of its supposedly assured second strike to defend the American homeland against attack, and *only* upon this means. Active defense against possible attacking Soviet missiles, whether by attacking them on the ground with American ICBMs or by intercepting them with ABM missiles, was ruled out as destabilizing. But if it would be suicidal for the Soviets to launch a strategic first strike against the continental United States, it would also be suicidal for the United States to resort to the use of ICBMs against the Soviet homeland. Consequently, it was no longer possible for the United States to threaten to launch ICBMs as the deterrent of last resort in the event of a Soviet attack on Western Europe. To do so would be to invite a devastating Soviet second strike against the American civilian population. Under the doctrine of mutually assured destruction, American intercontinental nuclear forces became political and military deadweight.

If the deterrent credibility of the third leg of the NATO triad could no longer be counted on, then the burden of defending Europe obviously had to be pushed forward to the first, and especially to the second leg of the triad. The possibility of using the American

ICBM force to bolster the second leg of the triad by directing its fire against Soviet and Warsaw Pact military assets rather than Soviet cities would also have to be considered. It was out of considerations such as these that both the Ford and the Carter Administrations announced ICBM retargetting policies during their tenure in office, and that the Carter and the Reagan Administrations have both strongly advocated the placement of the Pershing II missiles in Europe. And it was in order to frustrate the development of these options that the Soviet Union chose to develop its offensive missile power beyond the requirements of a secure second strike, to put the American Minuteman force in danger of a first strike, and to deploy the SS20s against Western Europe. Should hostilities break out in Europe, it must be assumed that the recourse to at least tactical nuclear weapons would come quickly, if not immediately. The Soviet Union would then be faced with the possibility of an American recourse to theatre nuclear weapons in the defense of Western Europe. With a first-strike capability against American ICBMs, the Soviets would be in a position to neutralize the Minuteman and to threaten a second strike against the continental United States if the American-controlled theatre nuclear forces were used against them. Or the Soviets might simply choose to prevent the use of American theatre or intercontinental nuclear forces in the defense of Europe by the simple expedient of destroying them before they are launched. Responsible European officials (not merely leftist radicals with an anti-American animus or Germans concerned with visiting relatives in the Eastern zone) must ponder the implications of this state of affairs.

Given the fact that the Soviet Union has approached this strategically commanding position within the terms of the SALT II Treaty, nothing could be more irrelevant to the security interests of the United States than the SALT II ratification debate in the Senate and its concern with parity—despite the fact that the parity question was generally raised by those who had come to believe that SALT was not serving the security interests of the United States. The debate over parity illustrates how concepts drawn from arms-control theory distract the public's attention from substantive questions of strategy by turning it toward spurious comparisons.

Conclusion

The considerations set forth above, drawn as they are from the logic of international relations and the experience of arms-control negotiations with the Soviet Union, lead ineluctably to the conclusion that the arms-control project cannot deliver mankind from the moral and strategic dilemma posed by nuclear arms. It cannot do so because it cannot address the more fundamental problem—indeed it must ignore the more fundamental problem—the prolonged international crisis caused by the revolutionary ambitions of the Soviet Union. However, two questions remain to be asked and answered in order to complete this discussion of the moral issues raised by nuclear war. The first question is, What purpose, if any, can arms-control agreements play in the contemporary world? The second is, Would moralists such as the outspoken American bishops be justified in branding a policy of nuclear deterrence as immoral *per se*?

In order to answer the first question, it is necessary to begin by observing that the relations between the United States and the Soviet Union have been essentially hostile since the end of the World War II. The arms competition between the two superpowers has substituted for the general war which such hostility would usually cause, but which neither antagonist feels it prudent to fight. If this analogy is accepted, then arms-control agreements can be seen as analogous to an armed truce in a hot war. In war, nations enter into truces when they come to believe that continuing the war, under conditions prevailing temporarily, would be either futile or exhausting. Thus the Soviets can be expected to enter into limited, but genuine arms-control agreements with the United States only if they see continued arms competition as inevitably bringing them disadvantage. It is for this reason that the Reagan Administration has decided to enter into arms-limitation talks with the Soviets only after it has begun its rearmament program. Any agreements thus reached, however, can be expected to be of limited scope and duration. They will certainly not be the "comprehensive" treaty expected by American policy makers at the beginning of the "SALT process."

In response to the second question posed above, it is possible to conclude that the reasoning behind the moralists' condemnation of nuclear deterrence is both uninformed and naive.

The moral case against deterrence can be resolved into two components. First, there is the claim that nuclear escalation cannot be controlled, that is, that the launching of any nuclear weapons, even at the lowest level of nuclear combat, will inevitably lead to a full nuclear exchange by the superpowers at all levels. The second part of the case against American deterrent policy involves the belief that deterrence can be achieved by nonnuclear means and that nonnuclear deterrence is preferrable to nuclear deterrence.

The first part of this case can be simply disposed of by observing that opinions on escalation constitute a judgment beyond the competence of moral teachers. The so-called "peace bishops" may be on sound grounds in teaching that there is no evil so great that one is justified in initiating a full nuclear exchange between the superpowers in order to resist it. They are out of their depths, however, in asserting that the launching of any nuclear weapons necessarily will result in such an exchange. The issue raised here is a highly technical one involving questions about the reliability of communications, command, and control facilities on a nuclear battlefield. The peace bishops do not speak with any special authority on this subject, and there is reason to believe that what they have said is ill-informed.

The second part of the case against American nuclear deterrent policy can be characterized as politically naive. Given the character of Soviet ambitions in Europe, the considerable strategic advantages conferred upon them by their forward position in East Germany, and the size of the conventional armed forces they have maintained, it is reasonable and prudent to suppose that in the absence of the American nuclear deterrent, Europe would have returned to the pattern of power politics that has characterized its past. One can readily imagine the Soviets initiating a series of military probes along the borders of their empire, as part of a strategy aiming at Soviet dominance of the Eurasian land mass and its adjacent seas. Without a nuclear deterrent to restrain Soviet adventures, the West would then be forced to resist Soviet strategtic thrusts by threatening the use of conventional arms. Threats of this nature clearly would have far less deterrent value than the threatened use of nuclear weapons, and therefore, it is likely that conventional deterrence would fail from time to time and that there would be periodic trials of strength between Soviet and Western arms. There is no guarantee that such limited wars would not escalate into general wars. Indeed, it is possible not only to imagine such a strategy of Soviet probes, but also to adduce actual instances of its attempted implementation. The Berlin blockade, and Soviet pressure against Iran and Turkey in the late 1940s, come readily to mind. Had it not been for the American nuclear deterrent, the chances are that war would have resulted from at least one of these crises. The casualties from such a war—a great power war—would have been heavy. That they have not been suffered to date is due to the fact that nuclear weapons have deterred a conventional great power war. Before condemning nuclear deterrence as a moral evil, therefore, the peace bishops shoud have asked which alternative is morally preferable: hypothetical casualties in a nuclear war, or real casualties in a great power war between East and West which would undoubtedly have occurred in the absence of nuclear deterrence?

Justice, War, and Active Defense
Angelo Codevilla

The assertion that nuclear war must be either mass murder or suicide, or both, cannot be founded on fact. Indeed, modern technology allows today's military planners, be they agressors or defenders, much latitude regarding the amount of damage they wish to endure and inflict—arguably as much latitude as the technology of any epoch has ever offered to the military planners living in it.

The arguments in favor of the assertion proceed from one often-stated premise: Nuclear weapons are so destructive that their use would be the end of mankind. According to this argument, nuclear weapons cannot be used to achieve rational objectives. In using nuclear weapons, no nation can prevent another nuclear-armed nation from devastating it. That is because, even if one power were to deliver a surprise attack on another's weapons, not all would be destroyed. Even the few remaining would be enough to destroy the attacker. Just one bomb will wipe a city—and more—from the face of the earth. Heretofore nations have entered into wars to achieve objectives that—evil though they might have been—were somehow grounded in the hope that life would be better after the war than before. But since the advent of nuclear weapons no such hopes are possible, since after war there would be no life at all. There would be neither winners nor losers—only dead people. War with nuclear weapons must always be senseless, and therefore unjust.

This situation cannot be ameliorated by means of defensive weapons. There are some 50,000 nuclear weapons in the world's arsenals. At one weapon per city, not only New York, Chicago, Los Angeles, Moscow, Leningrad, and Kiev would be incinerated, but also just about every center of population. Any attempt to defend the population is doomed in advance and for all time to come. At the cost of billions, an anti-missile defense might be built for a few metropolitan areas. The system might even be 99 percent effective. But even so, out of some two hundred weapons launched at a city, one would get through, and it would be enough. Such defenses might be all right for missile fields, where bombs landing would only reduce the number of retaliatory missiles available. But for each center of population, where one's enough, there can be no defense.

The mutual threat of nuclear destruction is perhaps the major cause of the enmity between the great powers today. Fear and mistrust, feed an arms race, feed upon themselves, and grow ever more dangerous to all. War is likelier today than in previous years *because* the superpowers have more weapons than ever before. Nuclear armament itself leads toward war. If the world is to move away from war, it will have to begin by reducing the number of nuclear weapons. This can be done without reducing safeguards to aggression because only a few hundred weapons at most on either side are enough for Mutual Assured Destruction.

The argument that I have outlined proceeds along mutually inconsistent lines. Only a few weapons are necessary and therefore morally acceptable for deterrence—a rational though distasteful purpose—because they would be used only in retaliation. Yet a few weapons can only begin to have some deterrent effect if they are targeted against centers of population. But the intentional, willing mass destruction of centers of population is, in and of itself, both irrational (since it serves no useful purpose) and immoral.

The argument, however, is protected by the claim that our situation is unprecedented, and that therefore neither the normal rules of argument nor the usual calculations regarding better and worse outcomes applies. On the one side we have nuclear weapons and the anihilation of mankind. Without knowing anything else, we instinctively feel that justice and morality must be sought in the other direction—at all costs.

This argument is wrong in principle and wrong as it relates to military strategy and technology. To say that "Our situation is unprecedented, for the destruction of the world is at stake" is hardly an unprecedented claim. Throughout the ages people have made the same argument to shield their claims from normal scrutiny, and to banish normal human skepticism toward outrageous suggestions. Catholics should remember particularly well the rhetoric of the several medievel chiliastic movements (Norman Cohn, *Pursuit of the Millenium*, Harper, 1963). The end of the world was at hand, they said. Therefore, a series of radical measures had to be undertaken which, incidentally, gave *them* the right to pronounce authoritatively on matters as diverse as economics and international affairs. To follow them and their counsel, prudence—the careful weighing of good sought, means employed, and results achieved—was to be cast aside. After all, the end of the world was at hand. These movements, we recall, gained substantial power, and led much of Europe to murderous strife. Many bishops, who at first were seduced into blessing these movements, were soon discredited and in many cases physically attacked by them. With this warning in mind let us look in some detail at the argument that the nuclear end of the world is upon us: first in principle and then as regards military technology.

Warfare Through History

The amount of destruction which men inflict on one another depends less on the weapons in their hands than on the intentions in their hearts and minds. History's cruelest battles have never proved to be nearly so destructive as the unobstructed dominance of cruel rulers. The worst slaughters have been accomplished without a fight. Just in the present century, the murder of six million Jews was accomplished wholly without weapons of mass destruction. People were rounded up, one by one, shipped to huge camps, and for the most part worked to death. The Nazis had borrowed the technique from the Soviet regime, which invented it— including its centerpiece, the daily ration earned by the daily work quota. How many have been murdered in the Gulags is not clear; the figure is between ten and twenty millions. The Cambodian communists took a mere two-and-a-half million innocent, unresisting lives in 1975-77, mostly by means of clubs and starvation. These are but the most egregious examples. One could go on *ad nauseam*. The point is that some kinds of "peace" are far worse than the worst armed conflicts, because the most murderous force in the world is neither the action nor fury against an enemy in battle, but the human desire to kill, regardless of innocence, and the unobstructed power to do so. The Jews of Europe, the millions in Russia, China, and Cambodia were killed not by gas, guns, clubs, and barbed wire, but by regimes that ruled those countries unchallenged by other armed forces.

Even in war, the degree of destruction is unrelated to the weapons used. Anyone acquainted with ancient history recalls that wars between cities, especially sieges, often involved ravaging the country (destruction of fruit trees, crops, and livestock), killing all the men, and selling the women and children into slavery. Sometimes the conquered cities themselves were demolished: *"Cartago delenda est."* Carthage was erased from the face of the earth by fire, sword, and the plow. Salt was spread over the earth to make sure that the land would remain inhospitable for many years. That was the rule then. The peoples untouched or little touched by our civilization have usually fought in this way, and do so still.

The common sense of philosophy, embodied in the Roman empire, moderated these ways somewhat. But not until Christianity had educated men to their universal responsibility—to do as much good and as little harm as possible in all various circumstances—were the horrors of warfare mitigated. The Church's guidelines regarding justice and war did not establish a utopia in which wars were eliminated or even in which all wars were just. People, after all, are sinful by nature. Jesus did not abolish sin. But, on the other hand, neither did the guidelines merely provide people with a new, hypocritical language by which to justify whatever they wanted to do. Through the middle ages, wars became less and less destructive—with one exception, the wars started by heretics who rejected, among many other teachings of the church, the teaching that the purpose of war is an arguably and proportionally more just and more secure peace. The heretics, instead, wanted to establish absolutely good utopias, and therefore felt justified in branding all who stood in their way, combatant and innocent alike, as absolutely deserving total destruction. That kind of warfare was not to be seen again in the West until 20th century utopian thinking once again caused men to forget the strictures of the church's fine distinctions. The Communists fought the Russian civil war less as a military campaign against the White armies than as war of annihilation against the social strata which might form a base of support for the old regime. The Nazis began to prepare the physical destruction of the Jews long before they planned World War II, and pursued their destruction even to the detriment of their military efforts.

During World War II the ratio of civilian to military casualties was about 20 to 1, largely because of the Allies' policy of strategic bombing. This bombing and firebombing of Tokyo, Osaka, Hamburg, Dresden, Berlin—which was grossly immoral—also turned out to have very little military value. The Soviet high command, not known for its scruples, and guilty of massacres from the beginning (Katyn forest) to the end (their end of operation Kellhaul) of the war, never bombed enemy cities. They were able to combine retail sanity with their wholesale madness. The Soviets did not have the bombs to waste, and kept the war's political purposes foremost in mind. Soviet military doctrine has remained thoroughly orthodox.

Strategic bombing could be termed a mere return to pre-Christian people-to-people warfare. There certainly was an element of post-Christian barbarism in it. But there was also a widespread utopian expectation among people that, if only Nazism and Japanese imperialism were wiped off the face of the earth, the world would live happily ever after. Absolute expectations or absolute fears—that is to say the attenuation of one's ties to the real world of relative evils, limited threats, and limited goals—tend to justify absolute abandonment of caution, proportion, and scruples. One tends to see one's self in exalted cosmic terms, as the agent—or victim—of history or of God.

When the first atom bombs were made, the U.S. was deeply engaged in strategic bombing. A single firebomb raid on Tokyo had already killed 135,000 people in one night. The bombing of Hiroshima, which killed about 80,000 people, was no more abhorrent than what had gone before. A debate began almost immediately in the U.S. How were the new weapons to be used? In the 1950s traditional military thinking seemed to prevail: nuclear weapons were to be treated like all others. They were to be made as accurate as possible (e.g. nuclear artillery shells) and would be directed against military targets. Collateral damage was to be limited both in the interest of military efficiency and of morality. Of course every measure was taken to protect the U.S. against the possibility that Soviet nuclear bombers might reach it. Fifty billion dollars (1950s dollars) were spent on Distant Early Warning Radars, and on the world's best surface-to-air missiles and interceptor aircraft. At the same time, however, the apocalyptic side of American military thought, mostly the former practictioners of strategic bombing, designed the Single Integrated Operations Plan (S.I.O.P.) to "bomb 'em back into the stone age." More important, this kind of thinking became associated with the proposition that because nuclear weapons had made war so terrible, large scale war could be banished forever. Would-be benefactors of mankind eagerly espoused the bloodthirsty plans of the Commander of the Strategic Air Command, General Curtis LeMay. Horror, wholesale destruction of civilians, came to be thought of as a positive good because, paradoxically, it was too terrible ever to happen. In the late 1960s and early 1970s Robert McNamara and Richard Nixon respectively committed the U.S. not just to destroying Russian civilians, but to keeping American civilians forever vulnerable to Soviet weapons. Only two key decisions need be mentioned: the Poseidon warhead was limited to only 40 kilotons and an accuracy of .3 nautical miles (NM), precisely so that it could be useful only for "city busting;" and the purpose of the American ABM system was changed from protection of cities to protection of missiles.

The Soviets, strictly for military reasons, have proceeded in the opposite direction. They have never targeted American population centers. Their weapons' yields and accuracies have tended to be designed optimally for destroying American missiles. Today, with accuracies of about .1 NM, their typical yields are about 1 megaton. Years ago, when accuracies were only about .5 NM, their yields ranged as high as 25 megatons. Either combination produces a high likelihood that American silos will be destroyed. Even when their weapons were few and inaccurate, they always aimed them at American military forces. They have also continued to build anti-air and anti-missile defenses, plus civil defense, to the best of their ability.

All of this is to say that the most important factor affecting the destructiveness of warfare, human design and preparation, is capable of aiming at very different results. We will see below just what results modern technology permits us to envision.

The question with regard to principle must be whether it is morally preferable to direct one's efforts toward mitigating the worst effects of warfare or whether it is morally preferable to try to make sure that any eventual war is as terrible as it could possibly be, in the hope that human beings will recoil from war altogether. Let me point out that the efforts which have led the West to its current vulnerability have not effected the Soviet side and therefore have given it practical leverage to work its will, and have tended to put the U.S., the world's *Defensor Pacis*, at a disadvantage. But even if we leave that point aside, we must note that no orthodox Christian thinker has ever attempted to justify any course of action which would reject lesser evils in favor of greater ones in the far-fetched hope that evil could be banished altogether. No orthodox argument can release people from the common-sense moral obligation to search as best they can, within the material limits in which they find themselves, for means to mitigate the consequences of war, and above all to make their own possible resort to war as just as can be.

Balance of Terror

As we have said, pistols, gas, and barbed wire—never mind fire-bombs—can kill millions. So can nuclear weapons. If one wishes to use them for that purpose, 50,000 nuclear devices are more than enough to kill every man, woman, and child on earth. Of course one would first have to gather the earth's population into groups conveniently sized and spaced and oblige them to stay there. In their natural dispersion, however, anything of the sort is far beyond the realm of possibility. This can be said confidently because the problem has been studied with a vengeance.

Robert McNamara very much wanted to be able to threaten "total destruction." But, as his experts simulated laying down nuclear weapons on Soviet cities, they found that, after the first 400 targets were struck and 25 percent of the Soviet people dead, striking every additional target would produce only an infinitesimal increase in casualties. The "flat part of the curve" had been reached; further effort was inefficient. Four hundred soft targets did not and do not mean 400 weapons. Most targets require far more. That is why our most numerous weapons, the Poseidon warhead, is so small and plentiful: the overpressures adequate for destroying buildings can be most efficiently spread over large areas by many small bombs laid down in a precise pattern. Typically, McNamara's targetting, using the roughly 4000 American weapons then expected to survive a Soviet first strike, produced 20 to 80 pounds per square inch (PSI) overpressure over the largest Russian cities. Note well that such targeting left unscathed the Soviet leadership, the Soviet strategic forces, and other key military targets all protected against several thousands of PSI's. Since McNamara's day, as knowledge of Soviet civil defenses increased (the Soviet Civil Defense Manual has been translated and is for sale from the U.S. Government Printing Office), it became clear that McNamara's targetting would not begin to destroy the civilian things the Soviets considered most important—valuable production machinery and trained personnel. A series of experiments by the Boeing Company (T.K. Jones and Scott Thompson, "Central War and Civil Defense," *Orbis*, October 1978) showed that machinery protected according to Soviet methods could withstand overpressures of many hundreds of pounds. To destroy Leningrad's industrial capacity, for example, would take 111 American warheads placed right on target. Shelters for production workers and their food, etc. are even harder. Even to knock down buildings is not a trivial matter. A one megaton weapon will knock down every building in roughly a 10 square mile area. New York City covers 350 square miles. Los Angeles, depending on how one defines it, covers about 2500 square miles. How many weapons would be needed to destroy its industrial capacity? The more one looks at "total destruction", the more criminally stupid it appears.

Even one nuclear weapon in an unprotected city would be disastrous. But disasters come in different sizes. It does no good to anyone to pretend that there would be no difference between the effect of one and the effect of 35 or 350 weapons; or that the effect of 350 weapons going off in a 900 square mile area on the high plains outside of Grand Forks, North Dakota, would be like that of 350 weapons filling a 2500 square mile pattern in the Los Angeles area. Most important, it is essential to realize that no one has the slightest rational military incentive to strike cities.

The most rational way for the Soviet Union to attack the U.S. would be to send about 3000 nuclear warheads (usually in pairs to ensure reliability) against our 1053 missile silos, about 50 other air force bases in the U.S. and Europe which house long range bombers, plus fewer than 400 command and control centers, and nuclear-weapons storage sites. Key intelligence targets like NSA at Ft. Meade, Maryland or the Satellite Control Facility at Sunnyvale, California would not be hit by nuclear weapons. Rather they could be sabotaged by rockets fired from trucks traveling on public highways. Our submarines in port could be blockaded there by nuclear mines. The ports themselves would not have to be struck. The places to be struck are well *outside* such minor centers of population as Great Falls, Montana, Grand Forks, North Dakota, and Cheyenne, Wyoming. The silos typically are 30 miles out of town. Even if everyone in these base towns were killed (which is unlikely given the weapons' accuracy) the immediate death toll would be less than two million (that figure would include striking the submarine ports)—a fraction of one percent of the U.S. population. The rest of the country would hear through the news media about the pattern of fallout. The damage that fallout would do would depend on the weather and on the precautions which the people in the cloud's path would take during the following ten days or so. In no case would the U.S. suffer the kind of devastation that Germany, Russia, and Japan suffered during World War II—unless the U.S. did something suicidally foolish.

After such an attack the U.S. would have lost all but 50 or so ICBMs, and all but a handful of bombers. Half of our 31 submarines would be blockaded in port and useless. Our technical means of intelligence collection would be largely useless. Our major weapons would be about 1500 city-busting warheads aboard Poseidon and Trident I submarines at sea. What would we do with them? If, in anger, we sent them against the top 400 Soviet cities, some would be picked off by the budding Soviet ABM system, but some would find their targets. They would cause great damage primarily to the people the Soviet government had chosen not to protect. Perhaps as many as 10 million would die. If we sent these weapons against Soviet 'hard' military targets, they would be largely wasted. A Poseidon warhead stands only about a 1-in-50 chance of destroying a Soviet silo. If we sent them against airfields or 'soft' military bases, they would do damage to buildings, but not to most tanks (which are hard enough to survive anything but direct hits) or to airplanes, which would be dispersed. We could hit ports with some effect. But we would cause many civilian casualties.

None of these options would in any significant way diminish the Soviets' ability to do us harm. After doing any of them, however, we would be wholly without major weapons. We would have shot our bolt. The Soviets would have some 5000 intercontinental or sub-launched warheads left, and could do with us as they wished—including punishing us severely for our useless destructiveness. If they gave free vent to vindictiveness, how could they use 5000 nuclear warheads? How would the less sanguine—and sanguinary— among them justify taking it easy on us? The thought is sobering. No, the only militarily, politically and morally reasonable option at that point would be to surrender a disarmed but lightly damaged U.S. to an unscathed and heavily armed Soviet Union.

The above-mentioned scenario is possible today. The strategic balance, however, is changing. Soviet offensive weapons are being modernized. The fifth generation of Soviet missiles is just at the beginning of its test phase. We can expect these new missiles to deliver more smaller warheads with even greater accuracy. That means that our forces will be vulnerable to an even smaller proportion of the Soviet arsenal, and that even less collateral damage would be caused by a Soviet attack on American weapons. Some of these new counterforce missiles will be mobile, and thus invulnerable to any counterforce missiles like the MX that *we* might build. In short, the Soviets are at least one generation ahead of us in offensive systems. The big change in the military situation, however, will come in the field of *defensive* weapons. As we will see, this is where technology is now leading.

Modern Defense Prospects

The Soviets, of course, have emphasized the defensive element of strategy ever since the days when Kotussoff fought Napoleon. In the 1950s the Soviets built a crude but big air defense system. But while the U.S. was dismantling its own defense systems, beginning in the 1960s the Soviets added layers of newer technology. Today the SA-2 air defense missile, of 1960 vintage, stands guard along with the SA-12, which incorporates the technology of the 1980s. In all, the Soviets have 10,000 air defense radars, 12,000 SAM launchers, and 2500 interceptor aircraft.

Defense against ballistic missiles requires high technology. The Soviets have lagged behind the U.S. in the technology, but have outdone us by far in its practical application. The system of ABM interceptors around Moscow was begun in 1965. The U.S. tried to convince the Soviets that this was a futile effort. Indeed, the Soviet ABM could have intercepted only a few incoming warheads. Still, the Soviets adamantly refused even to discuss limiting ABMs—until in 1967 and 1968 the U.S. tested what promised to be the Spartan-Sprint ABM system. As originally conceived, the system would have distinguished Soviet warheads from decoys, tracked them, divided them according to which could be engaged by each of the ABM sites, and transmitted to each ABM site the requisite information about the incoming warheads assigned to them. Each of these sites would then have sent up long-range, exoatmospheric interceptors (Spartans) and then short-range endoatmospheric ones (Sprints) to catch the warheads which got through. Spartan-Sprint—especially its data processing equipment—was a decade ahead of anything the Soviets had. Any given area under its protection could have been saturated by the attacker, but, overall, the system would have stopped well over four-fifths of an all-out attack, and a much higher proportion of a lesser attack. Soon after the American tests the Soviets completely switched their long-standing position and refused to talk of anything *but* banning ABMs.

Since the ABM treaty of 1972 the Soviets have built five very large phased-array radars on the perimeter of the populated part of the USSR. These are of a type suitable for managing an ABM battle, and feeding the necessary data to ABM sites. These sites themselves may be protected by ABMs. The computers in use are much more sophisticated than the ones they were using in the early 1970s —courtesy of transferred American technology. Meanwhile they have completed tests on the SH-4, a spartan-type interceptor, the SH-8, a sprint-type interceptor, and the flat-twin transportable missile-guidance radar. These three components can be mass produced without being noticed by anyone in the West. With the big radars in place, and a stockpile of the smaller components, the West could soon be confronted by the spectre of a Soviet Union, which already possesses a superior sword, acquiring a substantial element of an effective shield. This screen's effectiveness would depend on how many sites were deployed, and how heavy an American response would be. The better the Soviet counterforce attack, the lighter the American response could be. Consider that 1600 incoming submarine-launched warheads, coming into McNamara's 400 targets, would not make for very thick clouds—four weapons per target, spread out over half a continent. The defensive system would not have an impossible job.

Advancing technology is also providing any nation which wishes to take advantage of it with yet another element of ballistic missile defense. In order to see missile warheads (relatively small objects) hundreds of miles into space, radars must emit powerful pulses very, very close to one another. Heretofore, in order to do this the radars had to be rather large and distinctive. Their data processing equipment had to be more powerful than that for air defense radars. Yet today's microprocessors are so superior to those of even ten years ago that the performance needed for ABM purposes can now be routinely packed into air defense radars. Modern air-defense missiles, for their part, easily develop 100 G's of acceleration, just like ABMs. In short, the distinction between air defense and ballistic missile defense has lost whatever technical basis it had ten years ago. Any air-defense site which takes advantage of modern technology would be inherently capable of knocking down at least a few incoming warheads. The U.S. government confronted this fact almost a decade ago, when it began to build our first "modern" air-defense system, the Patriot. Back and forth the decision went: would the system be allowed to have an ABM capability or not? The system underwent three major redesigns. The last, under the Carter Administration, stripped it of its most modern features. There is no reason whatever to believe that the Soviet Union, in building its SA-11 and SA-12, has done similar violence to technology just to make sure it won't be able to protect itself.

Recent developments in the technology of space laser weapons promise not only a very significant attenuation of the threat from ballistic missiles and long-range bombers, but its virtual end.

The idea of defending the earth against ballistic missiles from orbiting platforms is not new. As early as 1960, the aerospace industry was working on rockets which would have been based in space and which would have homed in on the heat plumes of ballistic missiles during their boost phase. But the imprecision of those days' guidance technology meant that the rockets had to be armed with nuclear weapons. The U.S. abandoned this field in homage to Mutual Assured Destruction and out of a desire to keep nuclear weapons out of space. The Soviets did not do much in the field because they lacked the technology. Today, guidance technology has improved to the point that miniature homing vehicles in space do not even need an explosive warhead. They merely run into their targets at relative speeds of up to 30,000 miles per hour. Today also there is much interest in this field in both the U.S. and the Soviet Union. But, at the same time much more exciting work is going on in the field of lasers.

Lasers are beams of *coherent* light, light of a single frequency. Coherence increases the effect of a given amount of light by a factor of 100,000 to one. In 1978, a series of tests by the Lockheed company indicated that liquid-fueled missiles—such as the SS-17, SS-18, SS-19 —would be destroyed by as little as 100 watts per second per square centimeter (joules/cm^2) of high infrared laser light. To be safe one would want to irradiate them with more than 500 joules/cm^2. Even so, that is not a lot of energy. The emission of laser light can be stimulated by exciting certain molecules in gases or solids by electricity, combustion, or x-rays. The method which has recently been developed for space weapons involves combustion of pure hydrogen and pure fluorine. The combustion occurs in a small chamber. Its product, Hydrogen Fluoride (HF) gas escapes at hypersonic speeds through thousands of small nozzles into an area of very, very low pressure. There the HF molecules "snap back" and emit electromagnetic waves 2.7 microns long. These are drawn off by two concave mirrors, fashioned into a beam, and reflected against a large-beam director mirror, which then focuses against a target thousands of miles away.

This is anything but science fiction. The major pieces of the space laser weapon exist or are being built. There are three principal pieces: the laser device, the pointer-tracker, and the main mirror.

The laser device is being built by TRW and Rocketdyne in Los Angeles. Its core is a finely engineered metal cylinder which resembles a rocket engine, about three feet in diameter and fifteen feet long. In the test versions, the cylinder is surrounded by a vacuum chamber, which is fed by huge, steam-driven vacuum pumps. (This is necessary to draw exhaust gas out at hypersonic speeds.) In space, where the vacuum is more perfect, the device will function more efficiently, and will put out more power than in test versions. The cylinders now being built were designed to put out 5 megawatts of continuous-wave laser radiation. But finer designs may result in the production of 10 megawatts or more. The point to note here is that no external source of power, no Hoover Dam, is required to produce an awful lot of light. Rather, about 100 pounds of fuel may be enough to produce 10 million joules for a second—long enough to shoot down a missile thousands of miles away. Enough fuel for 400 or 500 seconds would be stored in cryogenic tanks. Building them is the speciality of Beech Aircraft in Denver, Colorado. This is not science fiction, nor even science—just solid engineering.

The pointer-tracker contract has gone to Lockheed, Palo Alto and Sunnyvale, California. This is not radically new technology. Lockheed had previously designed and built the Space Telescope, which points about as accurately and steadily as the space laser will. But whereas the telescope can take as much as a minute to find its target, the space laser must switch from target to target in less than a second. Whereas the telescope is virtually vibration-free, the laser generates lots of vibrations. On the other hand, though the telescope must sweep the heavens, the laser must only move a few degrees or less from target to target. Above all, the laser pointer-tracker can rely on a positive return of laser light coming back from the target to hold its point. At any rate, the basic technological issues in pointer-tracking were settled long ago. The rest is engineering.

The simplest technology in lasers is that of large mirrors. Eastman Kodak Company, producer of fine commercial optics, is building a machine to produce segments for large mirrors. Lockheed is building the control devices to align the edges very precisely and to modify the shape of the mirror ever so slightly to achieve a fine focus. Big mirrors, however, require big production facilities. Kodak is prepared to deliver the mirrors in quantity—but only after the expensive plants are built.

Laser systems require a variety of lesser but nonetheless vital pieces. Two examples will suffice. A system to insulate the laser's vibration from the vibration-free pointer-tracker and mirror is required. Two companies, Martin Marietta and Sperry Rand, have competing solutions. A computer program is needed to tell each laser station where it is in relation to every other station and in relation to every target, as well as to assign each target to a station in the most efficient order. Another program is needed to run the station's many housekeeping functions, from turning on the fuel pumps to modifying the shape of the small mirrors in the beam train to achieve a flat wave front. The miniaturized high capacity computer is no problem. But writing the complex programs takes time and forethought: e.g. under what conditions will the lasers be allowed to fire? Two unscheduled missile launches? Three? How far apart? And so on.

When will the very first laser station be launched? This year the U.S. Senate unanimously passed an amendment directing the Secretary of Defense to launch the first laser demonstrator weapon in this decade. This is hardly rushing things. In 1980 the Director of the Defense Advanced Research Projects Agency reported to the Congress that a weapon could be built by early 1987. Authorities in industry—the people who would actually do it—believe they could shorten the time significantly. Two different intelligence reports made public by the House of Representatives and by the *New York Times* (18 May 1980) tell us that the Soviets are expected to test their space laser weapon between 1983 and 1987. Since the American Defense bureaucracy, still intellectually stuck in Mutual Assured Destruction, is resisting laser weapons mightily, the Soviets are likely to test their's first. After all, their laser program is much larger than our own and, more important, is oriented toward achieving a real defensive capability. Perhaps, once the Soviets test their weapon, the bureaucratic resistance to American laser weapons will diminish.

When the first laser is launched, it will have the capability to destroy any object in space. Satellites are extremely soft, and the boosters which put them in orbit almost as soft. The nation which first puts a laser in orbit will be in a position to control entry into space during peacetime, telling other space users that the weapon automatically shoots new entries into space, and that registration of new satellites is required if they are to be spared. As few as four stations would allow their owner to defeat any fleet of long-range bombers. These, of course, must fly high during most of the intercontinental trip, and would be vulnerable for hours to repeated passes by the orbiting lasers. As few as ten stations would allow their owner to shield his country from submarine-launched ballistic missiles. These are a relatively easy problem for the lasers because they would be fired from widely separated parts of the globe and, in any case, they could not be fired in a salvo. About two dozen first-generation lasers of the kind whose components are now being built in the U.S. would be needed to have a reasonable chance of defeating an attack by large numbers of ICBMs. Computer studies have shown that a fleet of 24 ten-megawatt lasers fitted with ten meter main mirrors, with an accuracy of between .1 and .2 microradians would kill 2 Soviet ICBMs per second. If 1000 ICBMs (twice as many as would be launched in a counterforce attack) were launched over a five-minute period, all would likely have been shot down before the last missile launched had finished its boost phase (550 seconds later).

Obviously more missiles would be destroyed if more laser stations were deployed, and fewer would be destroyed if the deployment were smaller. The stations might work better than expected, as some weapons systems do, or they might not work so well, as some others do. However, even a minimally efficient American laser deployment would remove from the Soviet Union the temptation which it now faces, the condition which has brought the world closer to war. With the U.S. undefended, Soviet planners can figure arithmetically that over 90 percent of their warheads once launched would arrive on target and destroy the only force in the world they need fear. Moreover, they can count on doing it with less than half their force. Once enough American lasers were deployed to shoot down even half of a 500-missile attack, that attack could not succeed and would probably not be attempted. The mere existence of a defensive force turns an all-too-easy arithmetic calculation into a set of unanswerable questions: How many will the defense intercept? Which ones will be intercepted and therefore which targets will not be hit? Where will the unharmed American missiles be directed? The more such questions, the safer the peace.

Chemical laser weapons should not be thought of as ultimate weapons. Countermeasures can be taken against them as against any weapon. But such countermeasures will not be easy. Nuclear-tipped missiles could be fired at these stations. But even if these missiles were somehow not to be destroyed during boost phase, any terminal guidance mechanism could easily be burned out by the laser. If the warhead were to carry no guidance but rather were thickly armored against the lasers launched on a preset course to explode near the laser, a mere change of course by the laser would put it out of harm's way. A variety of other threats can also be dealt with. The comments (by Richard Garvin and Koska Tsipis) to the effect that laser weapons would be easily countermeasures are simply ill-informed. These men have never even talked with the engineers doing the work. For example, the assertion that Soviet missiles could easily be hardened to resist more than 20,000 joules/cm² is fantasy. The only materials which theoretically might withstand such fluxes don't have the structural properties to be used as missile skins. Ultimately, laser stations, like tanks, can be destroyed by similar devices which carry more power, more armor, or shoot first. After the lasers, God only knows what else will be invented.

There are not now and never will be any ultimate weapons. Again and again through the ages people have wanted to believe that some advance or another had made either the offense or the defense forever dominant, that military history had come to an end. But, history, military and otherwise, has not come to an end, and will not do so until God so decrees. In the meanwhile, men are obliged to do the best they can with what their minds and labors can produce.

Today we can see our way clear technologically to ending the era, now over twenty years old, during which nuclear offensive forces were thought to be dominant. On what moral ground could we hesitate to do so?

As citizens of a democracy, we know that our attitudes result in actions for which we are morally responsible. Should we have weapons capable of preventing the Soviet Union from achieving the ability to do as it wishes with our country and all others? If so, where should our offensive weapons be aimed: at apartment complexes or missile silos? If they are to aimed at missile silos, the purpose must be to destroy them, and the weapons ought to be designed so as to do that. Should our tax dollars, devoted to keeping the Soviets from doing their will, be spent on delivering nuclear weapons on Soviet soil; or should a portion be spent to try to keep Soviet warheads from landing here? If it is a worthy purpose to keep Soviet warheads from landing in the U.S., is the worthiness of that purpose diminished by the lack of assurance that we will be 100 percent successful forever?

It is essential to keep in mind that, although each of us is morally responsible for the answers we give and for the direction in which we push our country, these questions are not soluble in moral terms alone. These are questions best answered by prudence. But whereas a lively moral sense and moral reminders are of great assistance to prudent men trying to do the best they can, moralistic pronouncements based on utopian premises are about as antithetical to prudence as anything can be.

Traditional Western Criteria
for Justice in War

Most Rev. John J. O'Connor

Since I have been introduced as a member of the Bishops' Ad Hoc Committee on War and Peace, it is important that I begin with a disclaimer: I am not here representing the Committee. I shall not be addressing the contents of the proposed Pastoral Letter being prepared for the approval of the National Conference of Catholic Bishops, and, for the most part, I shall even avoid addressing the more critical issues one might expect the proposed document to address. Since it will be of interest to you, however, I am sure, I will tell you something of the procedure used by the Committee and the status of its efforts.

For approximately eighteen months the Committee has been taking testimony from a broad spectrum of witnesses: Administration officials, past and present, theologians, Scripture scholars, pacifists, military experts, medical doctors, and others. After extensive thinking, discussing, and praying together the Committee prepared and published a first draft of the proposed Pastoral Letter on War and Peace. Distributed to all the bishops of the United States and to a number of bishops elsewhere, as well as to the Holy Father, to various theologians and to all persons who had given testimony, this first draft brought many hundreds of commentaries.

The Committee proceeded to prepare a second draft, taking careful note of all commentaries, and including substantial reference to a crucial address by His Holiness, Pope John Paul II. This address, delivered by the Vatican's Secretary of State, His Eminence Cardinal Casaroli, to the Special Session on Disarmament at the United Nations (11 June 1982), was presented after the Committee's first draft had been completed, and was therefore not represented in the first draft.

The second draft of the proposed Pastoral, to be discussed by all the bishops of the United States at their annual conference in November of 1982, will be emended as required following discussion

Editor's note: Bishop O'Connor's remarks here were delivered before the November bishops' conference, and before the publication of the second draft of the pastoral letter.

by the bishops, comments by theologians and others, the recommendations of the Holy See, and the suggestions of the bishops of other lands. A third draft will be prepared by the Committee and submitted to the National Conference of Catholic Bishops some time after the November meeting. If approved by a two-thirds majority, the document will be published as a Pastoral Letter of the Bishops of the United States.

I turn now to the topic I have been asked to address: *Traditional Western Criteria for Justice in War.* Normally, one would be expected to address "Just War," under this title, and this I shall do, but rather indirectly. More immediately I intended to speak of certain underlying moral, ethical, religious, and particularly theological values and beliefs, those from which, it appears to me, Just War tradition is derived. Indeed, I have come to believe that Just War tradition can not really be understood divorced from these values and beliefs, and that much of the misunderstanding of Just War teaching is attributable to the failure to relate it to such. I believe it a mistake, and one all too common, to approach Just War tradition solely by way of the criteria to be met if war is to be considered "just." Rather obviously, for example, one has to have some understanding of what was meant by "justice" in the thinking of those who devised or developed such criteria. Justice, however, while crucial, is but one of the values basic to Just War tradition. We shall address it shortly, but we must first look at a fundamental theological teaching and religious belief in Christianity.

How I Try to Think About War and Peace

The central reality for Christianity throughout the ages has been the Resurrection of Jesus Christ with the potential for personal and individual resurrection it provides for all who "die in Christ." This life is at best a pilgrimage. "If our hope in Christ has been for this life only, we are the most unfortunate of people." (I Cor. 15:19) The Christian is to live with one foot on earth, one in heaven, where "This mortal body will be clothed with immortality" and death "swallowed up in victory." (1 Cor. 15:54-56) "The present burden of our trial is light enough, and earns for us an eternal weight of glory beyond all comparison. We do not fix our gaze on what is seen but on what is unseen. What is seen is transitory; what is unseen lasts forever . . . when the earthly tent in which we dwell is destroyed we have a dwelling provided for us by God, a dwelling in the heavens . . . to last forever. . . ." (2 Cor.)

Pauline and other scriptural texts could be multiplied, as could citations from early Church Fathers. The point would merely be verified and reemphasized that while human life—the life of every human person—is sacred because fashioned after the image and likeness of God, life *here* in *this* world is not the ultimate value or greatest of all values. Maximilian Kolbe, recently designated for canonization by Pope John Paul II, was considered saintly for many reasons, but certainly key to his canonization was his giving his life for that of a fellow prisoner of war. "Greater love than this no man has, than that he lay down his life for his friends." Christianity has never taught for a moment that life on this earth—precious though it is, and to be revered in every human being from the very first moment of conception to the final breath drawn—takes precedence over all other values. This was not the teaching given to early Christians. It is not what we teach today. Indeed, in Catholicism, since Vatican II we have reemphasized our basic belief by abandoning the term "Funeral Mass" in favor of "Mass of Resurrection," and the grieving are told of their loved ones who have died, "Life is changed, not ended."

To address other values underlying Just War, I turn to James Thurber's story of "The Bear Who Let It Alone," in his *Fables For Our Times*.

Thurber tells of a brown bear who lived in the woods, and who "could take it or let it alone." In due time, however, he began drinking heavily all day long; he would go home at night, smash up the furniture, and generally wreck the house, after which he would collapse on the floor and go to sleep. "His wife was greatly distressed," says Thurber, and his children very frightened.

Then the bear reformed, became a teetotaller and lecturer on alcoholism. He no longer went to the barroom, but would invite other bears to his house to tell them of the terrible effects of drink. To show how strong and healthy he had become since giving up drinking, he would do handstands and turn cartwheels, smashing up the furniture and generally wrecking the house. After such exercise, he would collapse on the floor and go to sleep. "His wife was greatly distressed," says Thurber, and his children very frightened. The moral Thurber gives? "You might as well fall flat on your face as lean over too far backward."

In human actions, good intentions are not enough. People with good intentions are quite capable of destroying the world or encouraging its destruction, through either excessive military action or complete passivity in response to aggression. Every act of defense, of preparation for war, of war itself, must be judged not only in terms of the intention of the act, but the circumstances involved, the net result that can be reasonably expected, and the nature of the act itself, since an "intrinsically evil" act may never be justified, however good and noble the intention may be or seem to be. Is the act balanced, that is, proportionate to what is required by justice?

In his first encyclical, The Redeemer of Man, Pope John Paul II warned:

> Already in the first half of this century, when various totalitarian-isms were developing, which, as is well known, led to the horrible catastrophe of war, the Church clearly outlined her position with regard to these regimes that to all appearances were acting for a higher good, namely the good of the state, while history was to show instead that the good in question was only that of a certain party, which had been identified with the state.[1]

Justice: Heart of Just War

Now to some observations on justice, a concept not unique, of course, to Christianity, deep-rooted in Natural Law tradition, treated eloquently by Cicero and the Stoics, passionately in such ancient Greek drama as *Antigone*, meticulously by Plato and Aristotle. That each individual receive his or her due—the justice of *human rights*. That each individual give to every other individual that which is his or her due—the justice of *human responsibilities*. But while such is inherent in the very "law of nature" itself, it is illuminated and vitalized by Christian understanding of the intrinsic worth and dignity of the human person, the sacredness of human life even on this earth, and the belief that we are brothers and sisters of Christ, adopted sons and daughters of the Father, through the mystery of the Redemption wrought by Christ. "The redemption of the world—is, at its deepest root, the fullness of justice in a human heart—the heart of the first-born Son—in order that it may become justice in the hearts of many human beings. . . ."[2] What we are talking about, then, is how both the individual and the common good—both important—must be kept in balance.

This notion of justice is indispensable to *any* consideration of the issues of war and peace, not only to discussion of Just War. "After all," says Pope John Paul II, "peace comes down to respect for man's inviolable rights—*Opus justitiae pax*—while war springs from the violation of these rights and brings with it still graver violations of them."[3]

One distinction, so basic that to risk taking it for granted is perilous for an understanding of justice, is the distinction made by Saint Thomas between an "act of man" and a "human act." To take a drink of water for the same reason as a lower animal does so, merely to satisfy thirst, is essentially an "act of man"; to offer a drink of water to another is a "human act." Acts of men are usually thought of as morally neutral, or "indifferent"; human acts are morally good or evil, with the morality determined by the nature of the act itself (constituting it "intrinsically" good or evil), the object of the act, the circumstances, and the end. Acts of war would be judged in accordance with these same determinants.

Of further significance to formulators of Just War tradition, both Catholic (as Saints Augustine and Thomas) and others (as Hugo Grotius), was a recognition of "order" as an ideal in the universe, in the individual affairs of human beings, and in society. To such, justice was the primary arbiter of order, safeguarded as well by the other moral virtues of prudence, fortitude, and temperance, which helped to assure that very "tranquility of order" that Augustine called peace. These are virtues, however, capable of and requiring development by "natural" means, including, for example, self-discipline. But Saint Thomas and other Christian theologians saw yet another set of virtues as *supernatural*, or divinely infused virtues: the "theological" virtues of faith, hope, and charity, or love. Understanding the role of these latter virtues is also crucial to understanding certain aspects of Just War tradition, and indispensable to the building and preservation of true peace. While Vatican II calls peace a work of justice, it goes on to point out that peace is also the fruit of love, which goes beyond what justice can achieve, and Pope John Paul II calls it a gift of God.

"Peace on earth, born of love for one's neighbor, is the sign and the effect of the peace of Christ that flows from God the Father. In his own person the incarnate Son, the Prince of Peace, reconciled all men to God through his death on the cross. In his human nature he destroyed hatred and restored unity to all mankind in one people and one body. Raised on high by the resurrection, he sent the Spirit of love into the hearts of men."[4]

Within the context of a value system rooted in such concepts, the principle so important to Saint Thomas, "*In medio stat virtus*," is not a call to mediocrity, but to *balance*, in judgment and in action: that balance, or *sense of proportion* without which the concept of Just War would be meaningless.

Peace Not Mere Absence of War

Again Vatican II reminds us: "*Peace is not the mere absence of war* or the simple maintenance of a balance of power between forces, nor can it be imposed at the dictate of absolute power. It is called, rightly and properly, *a work of justice*. It is the product of order, the order implanted in human society by its divine founder, to be realized in practice as men hunger and thirst for ever more perfect justice. The common good of the human race is subject to the eternal law as its primary principle, but its requirements keep changing with the passage of time. The result is that peace is never established finally and forever; the building up of peace has to go on all the time. Again, the human will is weak and wounded by sin; the search for peace therefore demands from each individual constant control of the passions, and from legitimate authority untiring vigilance. Even this is not enough. Peace here on earth can not be maintained unless the good of the human person is safeguarded, and men are willing to trust each other and share their riches of spirit and talent. If peace is to be established it is absolutely necessary to have a firm determination to respect other persons and peoples and their dignity, and to be zealous in the practice of brotherhood."

This integrity of balance clearly permeates the words of Joseph Cardinal Hoffner's address at the German Bishops Conference at Fulda, September 21, 1981.

> It does not promote the cause of peace if men fail to seek objective solutions to outstanding issues, and instead, if they become emotionally aroused. Among such emotionally inciting slogans are: "Peace at any price!", "Better Red than dead!", "Destroy what destroys you!", "Make peace without weapons!", "Unilateral disarmament!".
>
> In his Peace Message of December 8, 1967, Pope Paul VI declared: "We can not build peace on cries or slogans, which may indeed awaken a response, since they express a deep and genuine longing of mankind." But these cries and slogans serve to conceal, as unfortunately they have concealed, absence of a real spirit of peace, of truly peaceful intentions; or they hide destructive plans and purposes, or disguise partisan interests: The Pope warns against a purely "tactical" pacifism which anesthetizes opponents whom it plans to destroy, and erodes the sense of justice, duty, sacrifice in men's minds.

While pleading that we listen to every serious proposal for disarmament, Pope John Paul II warned against "the phenomenon of rhetoric", adding: "In an area already tense or fraught with unavoidable dangers, there is no place for exaggerated speech or threatening stances. Indulgence in rhetoric, in inflamed and impassioned vocabulary, in veiled threats and in scare tactics can only exacerbate a problem that needs sober and diligent examination."[5]

In this context, but with very great respect for all that is sincere in the "peace movement", and, indeed, grateful for the awareness and sense of urgency it has awakened, I see as particularly important the remarks of His Eminence, Agostino Cardinal Casaroli, Vatican Secretary of State: "I think that there can be peace movements which are really respectable because they show a real feeling of crowds, of big crowds. We see that it is too easy (however) to instrumentalize this movement for other purposes. So we are always careful not to encourage some way . . . to instrumentalize this movement. We respect the feeling that is especially (that of) the youth. We see that they are really sincere. But many times there are other people . . . trying to avail themselves of this sincere feeling to reach other goals."[6]

Finally, in his World Day of Peace Message of 1 January 1982, Pope John Paul carefully emphasized the critical need for balanced judgment that goes beyond rhetoric and mere intention, however noble.

> Although Christians put all their best energies into preventing war or stopping it, they do not deceive themselves about their ability to c:.use peace to triumph, nor about the effect of their efforts to this end . , .In the first place, Christians are aware that plans based on aggression, domination and the manipulation of others lurk in human hearts, and sometimes even secretly nourish human intentions, in spite of certain declarations or manifestations of a pacifist nature. For Christians know that in this world a totally and permanently peaceful human society is unfortunately a Utopia, and that idealogies that hold up that prospect as easily attainable are based on hopes that can not be realized, whatever the reason behind them. It is a question of a mistaken view of the human condition, a lack of application in considering the question as a whole; or it may be a case of evasion to calm fear, or in still other cases a matter of calculated self-interest. Christians are convinced, if only because they have learned from personal experience, that these deceptive hopes lead straight to the false peace of totalitarian regimes . . . This is why Christians, even as they strive to resist and prevent every form of warfare, have no hesitation in recalling that, in the name of an elementary requirement of justice, peoples have a right and even a duty to protect their existence and freedom by proportionate means against an unjust aggressor.

Or even, as the same Pope put it very simply: "There can be no love without justice!"

Moral Responsibility for Nuclear Arms

Jacob Bronowski was a dedicated proponent of value-free science. The story is told that following Nagasaki, he was asked by the United States to evaluate the effect of "the bomb". Coming in by small boat he arrived at the fleet landing, where a group of American sailors were singing the ditty of the day: *"Is You Is, or Is You Ain't My Baby?"* For Dr. Bronowski the ditty was meaningless, until he made his way around a little grove of trees and came upon the devastation. Shocked beyond belief, he then heard the words of the little nonsense song pounding in his ears: "Is You Is, or Is You Ain't My Baby?" Can there really be a science free of values? Can a scientist or anyone else simply probe the secrets of the universe, commit all his skills to the analysis and development of their findings, then simply turn such findings over to engineers and others, and wash his hands of all responsibility?

What has the Bronowski story to do with the positions taken by the Holy Father that we have been discussing and with values and beliefs underlying Just War tradition?

As we have seen, the Pope enjoins against "a mistaken view of the human condition." One of the earliest beliefs of Christianity germane to Just War tradition is the belief in Original Sin, that mysterious historical catastrophe that has left every one of us prone and vulnerable to evil. We can disavow all personal affection, affiliation, or responsibility for Original Sin, but disavowal does not exempt us from consequences shared by the entire human race, or from the obligation of trying to mitigate such consequences, both by our own human effort and by availing ourselves of divine assistance.

For the Christian, these are not mere pious aphorisms. They are the stuff of daily life, the essence of the Christian worldview.

The bombing of Hiroshima and Nagasaki introduced at least quantitative and perhaps qualitative originality into methods of waging war. As Pope John Paul II has put it: "In the past, it was possible to destroy a village, a town, a region, even a country. Now it is the whole planet that has come under threat." The question arose, he pointed out, that will never leave us again: Will this weapon, perfected and multiplied beyond measure, be used tomorrow? If so, would it not probably destroy the human family, its members and all the achievements of civilization?

In the same address at Hiroshima, on 25 February 1981, he reminds us that science and technology are the product of God-given human creativity, and have provided us a wonderful potential that is not neutral, since ". . . it can be used either for man's progress or for his degradation". He goes on, then, to spell out explicitly our individual and collective responsibilities in light of, and as a result of, what men did at Hiroshima and Nagasaki, even though we personally, individually or as a society of the present day, were not in fact responsible for developing or dropping "the bomb" on either city. The very fact of the destructive potential of nuclear weapons, he argues,

> . . .should finally compel everyone to face the basic moral consideration: from now on it is only through a conscious choice and through a deliberate policy that humanity can survive. The moral and political choice that faces us is that of putting all the resources of mind, science and culture at the service of peace and of the building up of a new

society, a society that will succeed in eliminating the causes of fratricidal wars by generously pursuing the total progress of each individual and of all humanity. Of course, individuals and societies are always exposed to the passions of greed and hate; but, as far as within us lies, let us try effectively to correct the social situation and structures that cause injustice and conflict.

The consequences and the implications of the bombs used at Hiroshima and Nagasaki affect everyone and are everyone's "baby". They will not go away anymore than the secret of nuclear weaponry itself will go away. They must be managed, their dangers and evils mitigated through human effort and divine assistance. Nor will it do to disavow our personal affection, affiliation and responsibility for the existence and potential of nuclear weapons, to cry to nations possessive of such, "a plague on all your houses", to wash our hands of their reality. Unlike individuals, who may perhaps reject all involvement with nuclear weapons, nations *must* face their reality, and bring to bear every conceivable resource to control and eventually, to the degree possible, negate their horrifying potential. What an individual may say or do in conscience is not always an option available to a state.

Once again Pope John Paul II speaks realistically

> Some people, even among those who were alive at the time of the events that we commemorate today, might prefer not to think about the horror of nuclear war and its dire consequences. Among those who have never personally experienced the reality of armed conflict between nations, some might wish to abandon the very possibility of nuclear war. Others might wish to regard nuclear capacity as an unavoidable means of maintaining a balance of power through a balance of terror. But there is no justification for not raising the question of the responsibility of each nation and each individual in the face of possible wars and of the nuclear threat.[7]

Is You Is, Or Is You Ain't My Baby?

Must We Disarm?

When the Pope speaks of the horror of nuclear war and its dire consequence, he is reflecting in part on a forecast provided him by scientists concerning the immediate and terrible effects of such a war. Among these effects:

— Death, by direct or delayed action to the explosions, of the population that might range from 50 to 200 million persons;
— A drastic reduction of food resources, caused by residual radioactivity over a wide extent of arable land;

— Dangerous genetic mutations, occurring in human beings, fauna and flaura;
— Considerable changes in the ozone layer in the atmosphere, which would expose man to major risks, harmful to his life;
— In a city stricken by a nuclear explosion the destruction of all urban services and the terror caused by the disaster would make it impossible to offer the inhabitants the slightest aid, creating a nightmarish apocalypse.
— Just two hundred of the fifty thousand nuclear bombs which it is estimated already exist, would be enough to destroy most of the large cities in the world. It is urgent, those scientists say, that the peoples should not close their eyes to what an atomic war can represent for mankind.[8]

In addition, the pope has spoken many times of the madness of the arms race, the deprivation of the poor because of the diversion of the world's resources into armaments, the perversion of certain sectors of the Third World through the purchase of arms, rather than through constructive aid, the grave dangers of accidental detonation of warheads, and related problems.

Yet given all the warnings, sensitive to all the dangers, and aware of all the controversies, what does the Holy Father say about the possession of nuclear arms in a world devoid of a world organization capable of assuring peace with justice for all people and of preserving that "tranquillity of order" required for such?

> ... the only choice that is morally and humanly valid, is represented by the reduction of nuclear armaments, while waiting for their future complete elimination, carried out simultaneously by all the parties, by means of explicit agreements and with the commitment of accepting effective controls.[9]

It seems hardly by inadvertence, given the context of this address that the Holy Father failed to condemn the *possession* of nuclear weapons.

Nor does it seem at all inadvertent, given the context — his address to the Special Session on Disarmament at the United Nations — that rather than condemning nuclear deterrence, either as intrinsically evil or because of attendent evils, the Holy Father stated:

> In current conditions "deterrence" based on balance, certainly not as an end in itself but as a step on the way toward a progressive disarmament, may still be judged morally acceptable.

How could the Holy Father maintain such a position, together with that of his January 1982 World Day of Peace Message previously referenced, except that he recognizes that peace can not exist in a vacuum, peace can not exist without justice, peace is not the mere absence of war; peace requires equity for all people; peace demands recognition of the worth and dignity of the human person; peace is predicated on the freedom to exercise human rights and carry out human responsibilities; peace is achievable only through the practice of the moral virtues of prudence, justice, fortitude, and temperance, and a gift from God that can not be divorced from the infused virtues of faith, hope, and charity; peace is possible only when it is recognized that neither peace on this earth nor life in this world is the highest of all goods.

Much of that tradition, as I understand it, is embodied in the words of the Second Vatican Council's *Pastoral Constitution on the Church in the Modern World.*

War has not ceased to be part of the human scene. As long as danger of war persists and there is no international authority with the necessary competence and power, governments cannot be denied the right of lawful self-defense, once all peace efforts have failed. State leaders and all who share the burdens of public administration have the duty to defend the interest of their people and to conduct such grave matters with a deep sense of responsibility. However, it is one thing to wage a war of self-defense; it is quite another to seek to impose domination on another nation. The possession of war potential does not justify the use of force for political or military objectives. Nor does the mere fact that war has unfortunately broken out mean that all is fair between the warring parties . . .

The development of armaments by modern science has immeasurably magnified the horrors and wickedness of war. Warfare conducted with these weapons can inflict immense and indiscriminate havoc which goes far beyond the bounds of legitimate defense, Indeed if the kind of weapons now stocked in the arsenals of the great powers were to be employed to the fullest, the result would only be the almost complete reciprocal slaughter of one side by the other, not to speak of the widespread devastation that would follow in the world and the deadly aftereffects resulting from the use of such arms . . .

Since peace must be born of mutual trust between peoples instead of being forced on nations through dread of arms, all must work to put an end to the arms race and make a real beginning of disarmament, not unilaterally indeed but at an equal rate on all sides, on the basis of agreements and backed up by genuine and effective guarantees.[10]

As I perceive it, Just War tradition evolved precisely to preserve peace thus defined, even if its definition is not explicated in such terms, or a systematic theology of peace consistently elaborated by way of the moral, ethical, religious, and theological values we have been discussing as the underpinnings of that tradition.

Just War Criteria

We come, then, although briefly, to the specific criteria traditional to Just War teaching inherent in this Vatican II statement, mindful once again, that these criteria are meaningful only in terms of the evaluation of human acts in their totality, including their very nature, and the object, circumstances, and end involved. The meaningfulness of Just War, too, is inseparable from concepts of balance, of justice, of proportion, of the conviction: *In medio stat virtus*. And Just War tradition is meaningful only if seen as an effort to achieve and preserve just peace, not to legitimize war as such. Finally, and most importantly, no one can understand the meaning of just war who does not understand the meaning of just peace.

We remarked that our comments on Just War criteria themselves will be brief, not because these criteria are unimportant — indeed, precisely because they *are* important. We simply can not give them here the time they merit. Moreover, these criteria have been treated with meticulous care by Georgetown University Professor William O'Brien, in his *Conduct of Just and Limited War*. No one serious about Just War tradition can overlook that text. For our purposes here, I will simply note some of the major criteria, commenting briefly here and there.

First, the classic distinction concerning the justice of waging war is that made between *Jus ad bellum* (the right or duty to undertake war), and *Jus in bello* (the means used to wage war), Historically there has been little difficulty in maintaining this distinction. In the nuclear age, the distinction tends to blur, particularly since some denounce the right to wage *any* war today because of the danger of provoking nuclear war, which would result in such horrors that the potential of their being used is sufficient to abrogate or suspend a nation's right to wage war altogether.

Next, it must be noted, of course, that war can be justified only in defense against unjust aggression. War of aggression can certainly not be justified. A preemptive strike made to forestall or prevent an aggressive attack is another question, and would require a careful examination of actual circumstances.

Justice requires that even response to unjust aggression must be proportionate to the nature of the aggression. I certainly may not kill a man caught in the act of simply stealing a penny from me. That would be a disproportionate response to "aggression". For a man to kill another who is about to kill his wife would hardly be a disproportionate response.

Question: Is it ever "proportionate" to use nuclear weapons in response to unjust aggression? Answer: What kind of nuclear weapons? What kind of unjust aggression? What are the probabilities for limiting the results of such use? How much damage would be caused? Would the "nuclear holocaust" be triggered? How many innocent lives would be lost?

This leads to the criterion called *discrimination*. In part this means that in any response to aggression, one must distinguish between combatants and non-combatants. How reliable and predictable is any weapon? Is it conceivable, for example, that biological and bacteriological weapons could discriminate among potential targets or victims?

In any response one must ask, too, about the probabilities of success. Is a clearly "suicidal" defense morally justifiable? Is it fair to pose the dilemma, "Better red or dead", and if so, is it lawful to risk the deaths of an entire population rather than surrender to conquest by an enemy that would impose a way of life clearly violative of the most crucial human rights? Once again, justice, balance, proportion are required for judgment.

Is war the only means available to defend against aggression, or is reasonable negotiation or some other appropriate resort still available?

Just War can be declared only by lawful authority. What constitutes such? What of revolution, of insurgency, and counter-insurgency?

Just War tradition forbids revenge, and requires that one must continue to love one's enemies even while at war with them. All is *not* fair in war. Acts of atrocity are never legitimate acts of war. This is one of the reasons why justice in both declaring war *(Jus ad bellum)* and in fighting was *(Jus in bello)* requires training and discipline in the natural moral virtues, proper formation of conscience of combat forces, and, in the final analysis, an excercise of the "supernatural" virtues of faith, hope, and charity, or love, which latter need brings us, of course, face to face with what we might fittingly call the "Jesus Dimension" in today's agonizing questions about war and peace, in general, and the applicability of Just War tradition in a nuclear age, in particular.

Can the Gospel of the Prince of Peace, can Jesus Himself, ever countenance war? "By this shall all men know that you are my followers, that you love one another." Or, "He, who lives by the sword, perishes by the sword." Do such texts, which could be multiplied, preclude the very possibility of Just War? Some would reply: Neither John the Baptist nor Jesus Himself ever condemned soldiers. On the contrary, John told them to be just; Jesus praised the faith of the centurion, and reminds us elsewhere: "Greater love than this no one has than to lay down his life for his friends." Paul, in turn, tells us: ". . . Not in vain does this lawful authority bear the sword: for he is the servant of God to execute wrath upon him that doth evil." (Romans 13, 1, 4). And to the argument that early Christians did not normally serve in the army because true Christians could not condone the use of force under any circumstances, it is answered with considerable evidence that some Christians *did* serve, and that there were many other reasons as well, why many did not.

But is the *thrust* of the Gospels that counts, and does that thrust so clearly evidence that mandate of love that with equal clarity it precludes for the Christian all possibility of Just War?

For me, the dilemma best comes into focus in the story of the Good Samaritan, seen as the examplar of love in his treatment of the man who fell among thieves, was beaten and left to die. What Jesus does not tell us is what the Good Samaritan should have done had he arrived while the beating was in progress.

There is no question in my mind about the critical importance of the "Jesus Dimension". I am simply not sure that it provides self-evident solutions to the problems of unjust aggression. Nor have I any questions that many good and sincere men and women of many nations would unilaterally disarm tomorrow, at whatever cost, if they truly believed that this is what Jesus clearly required them do do. Is there any purely human authority in this world prepared to tell them unconditionally, without hesitation, that this is what Jesus does indeed require? Is that same authority prepared to risk the potential disaster or the oppression of countless numbers of innocent people should such action be taken by the armed forces of the United States — or — apart from unilateral disarmament — should action be taken that would gravely weaken the defenses or the deterrent capacity of the United States?

In a provocative article, "Religion and National Security", in *International Security Review* (Summer 1982), James V. Schall quotes Professor Joseph Cropsey's *Public Philosophy and the Issue of Politics*.

> Professor Cropsey, I think, puts his finger on the heart of the problem, its intellectual heart, the one most absent from current intellectual discussions about nuclear defense.
>
> "It might be that we pay for peace by abject surrender. This is unthinkable. It is unthinkable because the argument in favor of doing so is based upon the premise that, morally and politically, nothing matters — nothing, that is, except survival. The proper name for this position is not philanthropic morality but nihilism without intestines. The fortified species of nihilism also argues that nothing matters — except success. We have lost contact with the human spirit if we can no longer sense the repulsiveness of nihilism and the depravity of it in its emasculated form. If nothing matters, then human life does not matter. (Who would mourn it?) If anything matters, it is the decency of life and the possible self-respect of men."

Is life here and now the greatest of all possible goods?

There were many studies made of the peculiar phenomenon of certain American prisoners of war in Korea. I believe that in some ways the most insightful was that done by William Lindsey White, reported in his *Captives of Korea.* Describing those prisoners who had not necessarily been the most seriously wounded, badly tortured, diseased, or suffering starvation, but who simply withdrew from their fellow prisoners, curled up into a fetal position, and died, he says: "Those who believed in Nothing died of nothing at all."

Footnotes

1. *The Redeemer of Man,* Encyclical Letter of Pope John Paul II, #17.

2. *ibid.,* #9.

3. *ibid.,* #17.

4. *Gaudium et Spes,* Documents of the Second Vatican Council, #78.

5. John Paul II, Address to the Special Session on Disarmament of the United Nations General Assembly, June 11, 1982.

6. Unofficial transcription of press conference held at the United Nations, New York, on June 8, 1982.

7. John Paul II, Address at Hiroshima, February 25, 1981.

8. John Paul II, World Day of Peace Message, January 1, 1980.

9. John Paul II, Angelus Message, December 13, 1981.

10. *Pastoral Constitution on the Church in the Modern World,* Documents of the Second Vatican Council, #78.

Further Readings

The literature on the morality of nuclear war is copious, and complex. The following bibliography includes a few works that bear special relevance to the topics discussed in this collection of essays.

Bukovsky, Vladimir. *The Peace Movement and the Soviet Union.* New York, Orwell Press, 1982.
    A short (57 pp.) booklet, developed from a *Commentary* article, detailing how the Kremlin manipulates Western desires for peace. Authored by a noted Soviet dissident, this is probably the classic statement of the problem.

Cooke, Terence Cardinal. "Letter of Defense;" *New York Times,* December 15, 1981.
    In the face of mounting controversy within the Church, Cardinal Cooke wrote to the servicemen for whom he serves as Military Vicar. The result is a clear, understandable analysis of Catholic teachings.

Cropsey, Joseph. "The Moral Basis of International Action;" *Political Philosophy and the Issues of Politics.* Chicago, University of Chicago Press, 1977.
    Quoted several times by the authors of this volume. This essay is a classic philosophical analysis of the moral questions involved in the fight against Communism.

Decter, Midge. "Has World War Three Already Begun;" *Imprimis,* April 1982.
    A stirring lecture, calling the West to recognize the life-and-death struggle in which—like it or not—we have been engaged.

Dougherty, James E. *How to Think About Arms Control and Disarmament.* New York. Crane Russak, 1973.

Dougherty is one of the outstanding living scholars of the Just War tradition, and this book provides a tested, sophisticated set of insights into the practical morality of disarmament campaigns.

Van Feldt, Elmer. "When to Turn the Other Cheek;" *Columbia,* April 1982.

An unusual political editorial in the pages of the influential magazine of the Knights of Columbus, standing clearly behind the need for a strong national defense.

Graham, Daniel O. *High Frontier: A New National Strategy.* Washington, The Heritage Foundation, 1982.

A dramatic new approach to national defense, featuring a space-based system of anti-missile defenses, which could revolutionize defense theory.

Himes, Kenneth R. "The Catholic Hierarchy and Nuclear Arms;" *Forum for Social Economics,* Winter 1981/82.

Prepared before the present controversy took on its emotional tone, this essay sketches the intellectual battlefield for the debate that followed when the American bishops took up the question in earnest.

Johnson, James Turner. *Just War Tradition and the Restraint of War.* Princeton, N.J., Princeton University Press, 1981.

Along, with William O'Brien's book (below), this constitutes the state-of-the-art in the development of the Just War tradition.

Lawler, Philip F. *The Bishops and the Bomb.* Washington, The Heritage Foundation, 1982.

Short (21 pp.) and readable, this is aimed for the general audience, as an explanation of how Just War theory points to a new, stronger national defense policy.

Luttwak, Edward. "How to Think About Nuclear Weapons;" *Commentary,* August 1982.

With extraordinary clarity, the author explains how so-called peace initiatives would multiply the dangers of a major conventional war in Europe.

Marzani, Carl. "The Vatican as a Left Ally?" *Monthly Review,* July-August, 1982.

The author, an avowed atheist and Marxist, interprets Vatican statements as potentially supporting his left-wing ideology. The interpretation is perverse; the marvel is that conservative analysts often accept that same perverse interpretation!

Murray, John Courtney. "The Uses of a Doctrine on the Uses of Force," *We Hold These Truths,* New York, Sheed and Ward, 1960.

One of the more noteworthy essays by the Jesuit theologian whose thinking helped shape the Vatican Council. An early formulation of the moral questions posed by nuclear weapons, this endures today.

Nagle, William J., editor. *Morality and Modern Warfare*. Baltimore, Helicon Press, 1960.
A collection of essays featuring the most influential American Catholic thinkers of our era: John Courtney Murray, William O'Brien, James Dougherty, and others.

Novak, Michael. "Arms and the Church," *Commentary*, March 1982.
Novak argues, compellingly, that the "peace bishops" have ignored the hard realities of the Cold War, and thereby contributed to a posture that might make peace less durable.

(Institute for Religion and Democracy) *Nuclear Freeze: A Study Guide for Churches*. Washington, I.R.D., 1982.
Short editorials and background information collated especially for the use of church-related study groups seeking a working understanding of the freeze proposals.

O'Brien, William. "The Peace Debate and American Catholics," *Washington Quarterly*, Spring 1982.
A concise, pointed summary of the moral issues. See also "From the University," in *Washington Quarterly* of Autumn 1982, where O'Brien debates his colleagues: Monika Hellwig, John Langan, James Schall, and Francis Winters.

_____. *The Conduct of Just and Limited War*. New York, Praeger, 1982.
O'Brien is probably the outstanding living expert on the Just War tradition, and this is his most ambitious product. Indispensable for the serious student of the tradition.

O'Connor, John J. *In Defense of Life*. Boston, St. Paul Editions, 1981.
A readable, lucid delineation of how Just War theory affects our defense posture. Doubly interesting because Bishop O'Connor is a member of the committee drafting the bishops' Pastoral Letter on the topic.

Pope John XXIII. *Pacem in Terris*. New York, Paulist Press, 1963.
A sweeping call for peace, this encyclical helped spark the present debate among Catholics. The first papal salvo against the arms race, it set the tone for statements that followed.

Pope John Paul II. "World Day of Peace Address," *L'Osservatore Romano* (English edition), January 1, 1982. And "Negotiation: Only

Realistic Solution; Message to Special Session of U.N. for Disarmament," *L'Osservatore Romano*, June 21, 1982.

Like his predecessors, John Paul unequivocally condemns the arms race, while leaving no doubt that nations have the right to self-defense. A powerful moral witness with a clear practical conscience.

Ramsey, Paul. *War and the Christian Conscience.* Durham, N.C., Duke Univ. Press, 1961.

A leading theologian approaches the Just War tradition from a non-Catholic perspective, with markedly similar results.

Schall, James V. *Church, State, and Society in the Thought of John Paul II.* Chicago, Franciscan Herald, 1982.

A useful guide to the thought of a very subtle theological theorist, and an antidote to much ideologically based interpretation.

_____. "The Defense of Right and Civilization," *Homiletic and Pastoral Review*, August, 1982.

Analyzing the history of papal teachings on modern warfare, Father Schall points out the clear limits to the pacifist position.

Shafarevich, Igor. *The Socialist Phenomenon.* New York, Harper & Row, 1980.

In one of the most important books of our time, a brilliant Soviet dissident traces the history of socialist thought, showing its growth from—and similarity to—an ancient tradition of heresies. One of the clearest descriptions of the moral stakes in our confrontation.

Solzhenitsyn, Aleksandr. "Addresses of June 30, 1975, and July 9, 1975, to AFL-CIO," Washington, American Federation of Labor, 1975.

Solzhenitsyn, too, provides a crystal-clear explanation of the stakes in our current battle. From one who has suffered within the system of communism, a cry for Western understanding and response.

Stanmeyer, William. "Toward a Moral Nuclear Strategy," *Policy Review*, #21, Summer 1982.

Written for the general audience, but relying heavily on the Catholic moral tradition and the current debate within the Church, this article suggests some solutions to our moral quandary.

Thatcher, Margaret. "Address to U.N. Disarmament Conference," *New York Times*, June 24, 1982.

The most forthright recent statement of the responsibilities for the West, provided by one of the West's most powerful leaders.

Teller, Edward. "Dangerous Myths About Nuclear Arms." *Reader's Digest*, November 1982.

Often described as the father of the hydrogen bomb, Teller has unassailable credentials as an expert on the effects of modern warfare. Here he punctures a number of false notions about nuclear defense.

Walzer, Michael. *Just and Unjust Wars*. New York, Basic Books, 1977.

Another analysis based on Just War standards—this time by America's foremost socialist theorist. Again, the results differ only mildly.

Weigel, George. *The Peace Bishops and the Arms Race*. Chicago, World Without War Council, 1982.

Possibly the best single guide for someone seeking a quick introduction, this 60-page booklet includes statements by the "peace bishops," a devastating critique, and further debate.